A Dog's Tale

The extraordinary story
of Sir Wagalot Knight

This book is dedicated to Gill and
John Dalley, without whose single
minded determination and
dedication to animals, the Soi Dog
hospitals would never have been
built... and I would not be alive.

Thank you from all we Soi Dogs.

An independent publication first printed in Great Britain in 2022.

© Guy Wrench

Published by StopEatingDogs.com

Designed by Duncan Taylor-Jones

Printed by BookPrintingUK

Photos: The majority of the photos in this book come from the Soi Dog photo library and my own collection. In an attempt to best tell this story, I have sourced some non-credited photos from the internet. If I have used one of your images without prior permission, please forgive me. My only excuse *(other than being a dog and not really understanding such matters)* is that I did it for my fellow dogs and cats and for no personal gain whatsoever.

Opinions: The opinions expressed in this book are those of the author and not necessarily those of Soi Dog.

Index

Official Mr Knight pawtograph

I used to have nightmares, indeed I still do, but now they are few and far between.

I consider myself to be a very lucky dog; possibly luckier than any dog in the world other than Fendi and my Uncle Boonrod.

This is my story.

Chapter 1

I am born

08 October 2015

I am born … and what an eventful experience that was! One minute I was all cosy and warm and enjoying the benefits of an automatic feeding machine and then suddenly, plop, I was out in the open and in something of a panic. To start with I couldn't breathe but then, suddenly, I could. I later discovered that pups like me are born in a sac of sorts and that my Ma had to tear it open with her teeth to enable me to breathe. She also nuzzled and licked me clean which felt very cosy and wonderfully comforting.

My Ma, I only ever knew her as Ma although I suppose her friends probably called her something else, was perfect. She fed me, she cleaned me and she protected me. Feeding was certainly a challenge. In theory it should have been simple as Ma had lots of teats and there was only one of me but, whenever I was hungry and tried to feed, I discovered lots of wriggly lumps in the way. They all seemed to smell a bit like me and Ma seemed to like them, so I assumed they were important, even though I didn't really know what they were. Being born was certainly proving to be an interesting experience … and possibly more difficult than I had ever imagined!

At first I couldn't see anything because we pups are born with our eyelids sealed, usually for two weeks or so. This didn't worry me as I didn't actually know what "seeing" was, although I did keep bumping my head on things which was a bit annoying (and painful!). After ten days my eyes opened and Wow, was that confusing. The first thing I saw was a huge, furry, four-legged monster coming towards me licking its lips. Crikey, I thought, I am hardly born and already I'm in trouble; but then I recognised my favourite smell in the world; this leviathan of a creature was my Ma. Well, that was a shock; I didn't really know what to expect and I had a feeling that I was quite small compared to most things, but Ma was huge, she absolutely towered over me. I had a good look at her, well a slightly blurry look if truth be told; "So this is what Ma looks like" I thought to myself. Then I noticed five other wriggly things, much smaller versions of my Ma. How odd, I thought … what strange looking creatures, these must be the things that get in the way when I try to feed. I had a nagging feeling that I was missing something important here, but for now all I was interested in was where I was …

It seems that we lived in a hut of sorts, well rather a broken wooden structure. I could see what I later discovered was "sky" through all four walls and the roof. The sky was very blue and in the middle of it was a round ball so bright that I couldn't look at it. Even to my untrained eye, our home didn't look very secure, but it was a roof (of sorts) over our heads and for that I was grateful. The ground was quite soft and in the background I could hear a whooshing / crashing noise. I was determined to explore and find our more but, much to my frustration, I realised that I hadn't yet learned to walk. For a young pup eager to "get up and go" this was something of a hurdle. So instead, I decided to investigate the wriggly things that had, from day one, rather interfered with my feeding habits.

Strangely, these "things" looked quite similar to my Ma, only very much smaller and rounder. Like Ma they had heads (eyes closed), a body, four legs and a strange sticky out thing which occasionally wagged from side to side. Like me, they didn't seem to be capable of anything in the way of structured movement ... hmmmm; "Like me, eh?". Suddenly it dawned on me that I too was one of these wriggly things, albeit an advanced form with open eyes. I was learning fast. My Ma was big and hairy, I was small and fairly immobile, there were five other wriggly things to contend with and we lived in a wooden hut. The sky was blue, the ground was soft and the world made funny whooshing sounds followed by strange crashing noises. I was young, I was naive and I was desperate to know more.

Chapter 2
Weeks three and four

Now that my eyes were open I felt that it was time to learn to walk. This turned out to be a somewhat painful experience and involved many bumps and scrapes as my little legs were rather wobbly and struggled to hold my growing body steady. However, by now I was very aware that I had competition in the form of my siblings and, being the first born, I was determined to lead the way and to set a good example.

Fortunately the ground was soft, as learning to walk was something of a challenge. After my first few falls, it occurred to me that maybe I should learn to stand first and then, when I had mastered this, I could start putting one paw in front of the other. Fortunately Ma was on hand to pick me up whenever I fell, although the first time this happened, I really did think that she was going to eat me. A big jaw grabbing you by the neck, however loving its owner, is always a worrying thing, but to be fair Ma was very gentle with me.

One day I became aware of a strange noise, which I was eventually to discover was human voices. I jumped up to peer through a crack in our hut wall, only to be pulled back by Ma who, much to my distress, was trembling all over. "Shhh" she indicated while she pulled me and my five siblings closer to her and started to lick us all. Happily we were all hungry and started to feed and, before we knew it, this new noise had disappeared. It was about then that I remembered that I had jumped up to see what this noise was and so had passed, without me noticing, my first controlled steps! I was delighted and, despite the somewhat tense atmosphere in our hut, I started to run around and shout "Look at me, I can walk, I can run" except my words came out as little grunts and whines instead. My excitement must have rubbed off, as Ma seemed to relax and I am sure I saw her smile. In reality my running was no more than a slow, somewhat unsteady walk, but it seemed awfully fast to me. And what's more, none of my siblings could walk, so I felt something of a trail blazer.

That evening, although we were all terribly young still, Ma explained humans to us. At this stage she didn't say much other than humans ruled the world and they did what they wanted, where they wanted and when they wanted. Some were kind and some were mean and it seemed to Ma that they didn't much respect each other, let alone the world that we all lived in. Apparently they did lots of really crazy things, like making products out of plastic and using these things only once, then throwing them away. They also drove metal boxes on wheels very fast and ran over and killed lots of dogs and cats, and even their own kind. None of this made any sense to me as I didn't know what plastic was, nor metal boxes on wheels for that matter; but it worried my Ma, so I knew it had to be bad. Even worse, some humans hated us dogs and killed us with poison, or traps or weapons. This made for a poor night's sleep and more than once I awoke with a shiver of fear. What if humans found our little hut? I tried to put this thought out of my mind.

My life of discovery took an interesting turn the following day. When I woke up I felt sure that I must have drunk too much milk the day before, as I was leaking from a rather small looking tail between my legs which, to be honest, I hadn't noticed before. "How odd" I thought and, without thinking much about it, I got up and walked to the corner of our hut and relieved myself of my previous day's excess. I then returned to study my siblings a bit more closely. They were all a bit smaller than me which, of course, made them very small indeed, but only three of them had the same, funny looking extra tail that I had. In time I came to understand that there are two types of dogs, boy dogs and girl dogs, but for now I was just worried that two of my siblings might have lost their extra tails.

By now all we puppies were up and about and beginning to find our independence. One of us boy dogs was very small compared to the rest of us and seemed to stumble and fall a lot. I had so much on my mind, and so much to learn about the world, that I didn't take much notice of this until he disappeared. At the time I had no idea what had happened to him, but now I realise that he must have died. Ma didn't seem too sad to me, but life as a street dog is tough as I was learning, and I have no doubt that Ma had her paws full just keeping herself and the rest of us alive. I have since learned from experience that street dogs, if very hungry, sometimes eat their dead, but there was no sign of this in our hut and we just got on with our lives as normal.

My siblings clearly saw me as their leader as they constantly followed me around and copied me, although if truth be told, all I was doing was running around our hut in circles. We played rough and tumble together and jumped on each other and often onto Ma when she lay down for a rest; it was so much fun, or so it seemed to us. I think we must have all been about a month into our lives when Ma said: "Today we are going outside and you must promise to stay by my side. If I say Shhh it is because I feel danger in the air. You must do exactly what I tell you." She then went on to tell us that the outside world, as in outside of our hut, could be very dangerous and that we had to be vigilant all the time.

Well, I cannot tell you how excited I was! All my life I had heard this whoosh-crash noise and today, perhaps, I was going to see what it was. It didn't frighten me as by now, I was used to it, but I was intrigued. To get out of our hut Ma had to lift us by the nape of our necks and drop us over a barrier of sorts on to the ground outside, which was not a very dignified introduction to the world, but I didn't worry because what I saw took my breath away. I never, ever imagined the world to be so big! Directly outside our hut the ground was covered in green plants which made it a little bit difficult to walk, but this was not what had caught my eye. What I was looking at was a forever landscape of blue which Ma told me was the sea. She didn't really know what the sea was, nor what it did, but she did say we could play in it as long as we only paddled up to our paws and that we didn't drink it. "Drink the sea?" I thought to myself, "You'd have to be HUGE to drink the sea. What a funny thing to say!"

So off we set, me and my brothers and sisters, with Ma in tow, to explore the sea. Much to my surprise, as we got closer, I noticed that the sea moved. It drew away from us with a whooshing noise and then rolled over and raced back with a crash! Whoosh-crash, so it was the sea that I had been hearing all my life! One of life's great mysteries was solved and I was just about to go for my first paddle when, suddenly, Ma hissed "Shhh" and we all froze. In the distance were some humans walking towards us. After a minute Ma relaxed and said "Farang" which I was to discover was our word for foreigners or tourists. All the same we raced home to our hut where Ma told us more about humans.

Chapter 3

Three species of humans

Ma categorised humans into three groups; mean, indifferent and kind. As a dog, albeit a young dog, who had never done any harm to anyone or anything, I was shocked to hear that there were mean humans who purposefully tried to harm and kill us. Ma had mentioned this to us before and I hadn't fully understood, but this time she made it very clear to us that we would have to spend the whole of our lives assuming that humans were mean unless they had proved otherwise. She told us that many of her friends had died. Some had been poisoned, some had been attacked with machetes, some had been caught in traps and then killed and some pups she knew had been tied up in plastic bags and dropped onto busy roads where they had been run over and squashed.

This really put the shivers up us as it seemed so horribly cruel and unfair, but Ma told us that it happened every day all across Asia and she begged us to be careful. Up to this stage (although I was only one month old) my life had been something of a holiday, but I was beginning to realise that I had led a very sheltered existence and that the older I got, the more difficult life would become. I knew that the time was fast approaching for me to venture out on my own and that soon I would have to move on from the safety of Ma and our hut and this really scared me.

Next Ma described the indifferent humans. These were people who, in the main, just ignored us. This sounded good to me, but Ma said not to be fooled as they were still dangerous. Those who didn't care wouldn't always stop if we were in the road and they wouldn't protect us from the mean humans. Worse still, they could become mean humans if we annoyed them, even unintentionally, by barking outside their house for example. This was not looking good and I began to wonder what chances we would all have of living a long life.

Fortunately, there were also kind humans and there seemed to be lots of these. Ma explained that Thailand was a Buddhist nation and that, in general, Buddhists did not eat meat, because (1) the killing of animals violated the First Moral Precept of Buddhism and (2) meat is considered an intoxicant to the body, which violated the Fifth Moral Precept of Buddhism. I didn't completely follow this, but it sounded encouraging.

However, Ma went on to explain that some Buddhists did eat meat, especially when they themselves didn't kill it, and that not everyone in Thailand was a Buddhist. Ma continued to say that it was not uncommon for a Buddhist to ask a non-Buddhist to kill an animal for them, so that they could eat it. By now we pups were totally confused but Ma also told us that many restaurants, cafés, street markets and hotels left out waste food for us stray dogs and that we could usually find a meal at a Buddhist temple, as the monks were so very kind. She also said that there were 'shelters' for stray dogs and that the kind humans who ran these often drove around feeding dogs from the back of vans or pick-up trucks.

Despite her summary of kind humans, it was clear that Ma was very scared of all humans and this fear certainly rubbed off onto we pups. "Hmmm", I thought to myself, "It might just be easier to avoid humans altogether." Little did I know, at the time, that one day mean humans would try to kill me, that indifferent humans would rescue me and that kind humans would save my life ... but I am jumping ahead of myself!

Chapter 4
Growing up in adversity

We pups were growing up fast. We played together all the time, our favourite game being mock fighting. By now our teeth had grown so this could be painful, but the rule was, if one of us yelped, the other stopped biting. In addition, we were spending more and more time outside of our hut, occasionally even sleeping outside, and we started to meet other dogs. Initially this was a bit overwhelming, not least for myself as I had assumed the role of pack leader among my siblings (after Ma of course) and was rather enjoying being the boss. Suddenly, there we were face to face with other dogs, some even bigger than Ma, and we quickly learned to back away if a bigger dog growled at us, or even showed its teeth.

Life as a street dog bears no similarity to that of a pet dog. We live outside, we have no one to protect us and every single day is a challenge to survive. There are no let ups. Finding food, avoiding being hit by cars and motor scooters, running from bigger dogs, hiding from mean humans and being careful of traps are all tough realities. As well as this we needed to avoid the temptation of raiding farms to steal chickens ... knowing that the farmers will kill us if they catch us.

By now we were all on solid food and our diet consisted mostly of food waste, with the occasional wildlife kill (chickens, snakes, birds, rats, geckos, squirrels, frogs and even the occasional cat); or rather the leftovers of these kills if the bigger dogs left anything behind. Although we occasionally saw Ma, we were no longer living in our hut as it was impossible for Ma to feed and care for us now that we were bigger.

Before we had left, Ma had taken us out and about and showed us how and where to find food. To be honest, it was a miserable business that principally involved rummaging through bins and rubbish tips. Fortunately, as I was discovering, humans are very wasteful and throw away huge volumes of food, most of which we can eat. Despite this, I was hungry almost all the time as I was competing with other dogs for every scrap of food. One thing Ma taught us was not to eat cooked meat bones, as fragments could get stuck in our throats, or worse still, in our guts; but often hunger over-ruled sensibility and through desperation I would find myself in a fight over a partially eaten chicken wing or a scrap of carcass.

Every day was unique, as new challenges presented themselves. In theory being a street dog sounds easy; all you do is hunt, eat and sleep on a cycle. In reality we street dogs faced danger every single day and few of us lived to see old age.

Chapter 5

A day in the life of a street dog

I am a "soi" dog, soi being the Thai word for street or alley; ie the streets and alleyways are my home. As I have said, there is no such thing as a typical day, but if I had to describe an average day, it would be something like this:

Hunt, eat, sleep ... hunt, eat, sleep ... repeat. I have to pick carefully where I sleep. On the beach, in the woods, down a quiet alleyway, maybe on a pavement or in a derelict building. Sometimes around the back of a restaurant owned by a friendly human. Under a car or truck. What I mustn't do is sleep in places where humans do not like dogs or where I am considered "in the way" as humans call it. Sometimes exhaustion takes over and I bed down in the wrong place. When this happens I usually get a rude awakening, for example by having water thrown over me or stones thrown at me. One day I was woken by two humans beating me with sticks. Maybe this was my fault, as the soft grass I had slept on was in their garden, but I never meant them any harm.

Most of my day is devoted to feeding and keeping out of trouble; and in the hot summer, finding clean water to drink and shade to rest under. Sometimes I am lucky and I find a pile of unwanted human food that no other dog has spotted, but this is very rare. When it happens, I eat and eat until I am full, as it might be a few days until I find another proper meal.

Many a time, I find myself squabbling over scraps of food. I consider myself quite gentle by nature and the concept of fighting for food waste should be alien to me, but if I don't, then I starve. It is the same for all we soi dogs, which is why so many of us are scarred, we often have to fight to keep our food. It is a tough life. Needless to say, I use my discretion in such altercations. I am lucky to be quick on my paws, so more often than not I can escape with food in my mouth and run until I find a safe spot to stop and eat it. That said, I have been bitten and I have even delivered a few bites in my time. It really is a case of survival of the fittest and the smartest.

Humans think of us as pack animals and to an extent we are, but most of we street dogs hunt for food by ourselves. Maybe in the "bush" our ancestors and cousins hunted in a pack but, where I live, we tend to do our own thing. I guess hunting down a half eaten beef burger is somewhat different to hunting a live animal and, while I occasionally eat fresh meat, most of my meals are human left-overs.

Some days are easier than others. I remember one day watching a family from afar, eating a picnic down on the beach. They tried to tempt me over by throwing morsels of food in my direction, but I remembered what my Ma had said about humans and I kept my distance.

Eventually one of the smaller humans, I think you call them children, stood up and walked my way with a handful of food. Needless to say, I ran away but he simply laid the food down where I had been sitting. He did this two more times before rejoining his family.

After a while, driven by hunger, I returned to my spot on the beach and tentatively sniffed this offering and, before I knew it, I had eaten the lot! Whatever it was made me feel thirsty and, being on the beach, I went down to the sea to lap up some water.

Suddenly I heard the human shouting, what they were saying I don't know, but whatever it was it seemed to be aimed at me. Then the same small human got up with a bowl which he placed on the ground close to where I had been sitting. He then filled the bowl with liquid from a bottle and again, walked away.

Tentatively I returned to my spot and, to my delight, I discovered that the bowl was full of clear water. Not salty water nor muddy water, but clean, clear water ... I could even see the bottom of the bowl through it. It was delicious.

I mention this story to emphasise that there really are kind humans, indeed there are many kind humans in Thailand, but they do all look the same to us (two legs and two arms joined by a body with a head up at the top), so it is difficult to differentiate between mean, indifferent and kind humans. Which is frightening as mean humans often put out poisoned food to kill dogs. Taking food from humans is a gamble, but a hungry dog is a desperate dog and sometimes we just have to chance it.

Later on that same day, I saw two humans walking with a dog at the end of a rope (I had seen this many times before) and I allowed myself to pass quite close to them. It seemed to me that the dog gave me a friendly wink and this caught me off guard as one of the humans suddenly lashed out with a stick and delivered a horribly painful blow to my rear end. As he did so he shouted "Get away you filthy dog, stay away from our Millie." Millie, if this was indeed the dog's name, looked shocked but I knew my place and I made a quick exit.

In an instant, the pleasurable memory of my earlier encounter with humans on the beach was annulled and in some discomfort, I limped back to the beach where I found a quiet spot in the shade to rest.

Sometimes humans come up to us with food in their hands, tempting us to eat from them. I have never done this, but I have seen soi dogs sit with humans and the humans have fed them and stroked them and tickled their ears and been very kind. This looks such fun to me and I often find myself pondering mean humans' anger and hatred of we dogs. It is something that I don't understand and some days it makes me very sad indeed.

Another struggle for street dogs, especially in the summer, is finding regular clean water to drink. In reality, most of us drink from filthy puddles or, when desperate, from the sea. This is one of the reasons that the average lifespan of a street dog is often less than that of a pet dog; our internal organs struggle to filter all the waste we consume and, as a result, they can be prone to failure in mid-life.

In the wet season, drinking clean water is never a problem as the rain in Thailand, where I lived, is torrential. In fact it is so heavy that it creates issues of its own. We are often wet for days on end and, in the north, it can get very cold in the winter months. Many of the weaker dogs die as they are not strong enough to fend off diseases. There is also a lot of flooding and in extreme cases, this can kill many dogs.

My Ma always told me to spend that little bit more time finding somewhere safe to sleep and I am glad that I do this as I have seen dogs sleeping on the roadside which often leads to being killed. Likewise, I have seen dogs sheltering in drains and getting trapped in flood water and being washed away.

Those of us that survive the hardship of street life become tough old dogs, we have to. This is not to say that we do not sometimes have fun. The freedom of running unencumbered by a leash, of going where we want to go and of being part of a pack is truly exhilarating. We try and live every day to the full as we know that any and every day might be our last.

Chapter 6

Once we were wolves

At this stage, it might be worth exploring the nature of man's relationship with dogs. I understand that we are often known as "Man's best friend" which is strange when you consider the bigger picture. But more of that later.

Once upon a time, there were no dogs in the world. I find this hard to believe, but dogs older and wiser than me have assured me that it is true. But there were lots of wolves, not the grey wolves that we see today but an altogether more fearsome animal. Man rather admired these wolves as they were strong, good hunters and very capable of looking after themselves.

It may have taken a few thousand years but, in time, man decided that wolves would make good working animals and maybe even good companions. Or did they? Some think that mankind domesticated wolves, others think that the wolves themselves decided to co-exist in close harmony with man. As a street dog who spent the first three years of his life hunting down and fighting for every meal; and who is now served two delicious meals every day by my human; I can understand both arguments!

Of course, we'll never know when wolves morphed into dogs but we do know that the oldest known dog burial is from 14,200 years ago, suggesting that dogs were firmly installed as man's best friend by then. Science magazine estimates that wolves were first domesticated some 15,000 to 30,000 years ago ... based on rock and cave art ... so we have been around in dog mode for quite some time now!

Genetic evidence supports these dates and quite certainly man raised puppies well before he raised kittens or chickens; before he herded cows, goats, pigs and sheep; even before he planted rice, wheat, barley and corn.

Pugs and poodles may not look much like wolves, but if you trace their ancestry far enough back in time, even they quite definitely descended from wolves. I once spoke with my dear pug friend Rocky about this (we'll meet Rocky later on in my story) and he laughed at the thought of once being a wolf, or rather grunted as pugs can't breathe properly. I love pugs and I regularly meet a pack of six in my new life, but it saddens me that man should purposely breed an animal so far from its natural state that it spends its whole life gasping for breath.

No one knows whereabouts man and wolf-dog first became such good friends. Indeed, genetic studies have pinpointed everywhere from southern China to Mongolia to Europe. As an Asian street dog, I'd put my bones on Mongolia, but who knows?

What we do know is that the world's dog population is now out of control. There are an estimated 600,000,000 (yes, six hundred million) stray dogs on the planet. Some 5,000 beautiful, healthy, domesticated, pet dogs are destroyed every day in shelters around the world, having been left there (ie dumped) by humans. And yet mankind continues to breed and sell dogs to make money for themselves. It makes no sense at all ...

My human is always saying #adoptdontshop to anyone who will listen and I agree.

Just recently, in my new life, I watched a programme on the evolution of wolf to dog, although strangely the experiment was conducted using silver foxes. In this programme, which I did not enjoy as it involved capturing and caging wild animals, humans discovered that you could domesticate foxes in just six generations by selecting and mating the most "friendly" of the wild (and subsequently less wild) foxes. So, six generations on from catching a wild fox, that fox's offspring were sitting on the laps of humans and being tickled.

I cannot imagine that we "wolves" were that easy to tame and I truly hope that man does not continue to tame wild animals as it is not natural. We dogs are lucky, it has worked for us, but for every happy, healthy pet dog, there are many more struggling for survival; but without the survival instincts that our wolf ancestors once had. In the words of the anthropologist Brian Hare:

"The domestication of dogs was one of the most extraordinary events in human history."

Who am I to disagree?

Many woofs to Smithsonian magazine and Science magazine for help with this chapter.

Chapter 7

What's in a name?

Confession time! This chapter is a bit of fun as we dogs enjoy entertaining our humans.

The astute among you will know that we dogs have no way of knowing who our fathers are (ps: I hope you're reading this Sosay; #whosthedaddy indeed!) to say nothing of my grandparents. But if I did, this could be my back-story:-

When I was young my father used to regale me with stories about his parents and his life as a young puppy. My grandfather was called Mid Knight which I found rather confusing. At first I assumed it was because he was neither big nor small, but in time I learned that it was because he was born in the middle of the night. This confusion was caused by something called Google Translate. We dogs are good at translating smell and movement but translating Woof to English is somewhat beyond us. After all, even humans make mistakes! My father, incidentally, was called Good Knight, because he was a good pup called Knight. Despite being a Knight, one of my sisters was called Chocolate because she was born just after eight. As I said, it is all rather complicated!

Whenever my grandfather went to sleep, my father would say "good night Mid Knight". Sometimes, if my grandfather stayed up late, my father would say "It's midnight Mid Knight and time to say good night" to which my grandfather would reply, "Good point Good Knight, it is midnight. Good night". These conversations always amused me!

My Ma should have been called Ma Knight but my grandmother had a lisp, so Ma Knight became Marmite. Some dogs liked her, others didn't; but I loved her very much. Sometimes my grandmother would say: "What would you like for dinner, Marmite?" and my father would say: "Don't be daft, we've run out of bread". It is fair to say, our names didn't really help us in life.

Going back in time, one day (a good day for me as it turned out), Good Knight met Marmite and not long after (66 days to be precise), Mr Knight (me) was born. My grandmother declared this day to be another good day, saying that Good Knight was a good sort. Then, one night, Good Knight snuck off never to be seen again, and thereafter we referred to him as Good Riddance. Actually, my grandmother called him something else, but made me promise never to repeat the word!

In reality, of course, none of us had names, as none of us had humans to give us names. I spent the first three years of my life in a state of anonymity, I was just a street dog, one of 600,000,000 in the world, trying desperately to survive.

And then I had my terrible accident and found myself in intensive care where, for the first time in my life, I was surrounded by humans and with no means of escape. That's when I first heard the name Knight. Not Good Knight, not Mid Knight, nor Marmite ... just Knight.

"He's such a brave knight", I heard a human say ... and the name stuck!

Chapter 8

Living in a hostile world

I seem to be jumping ahead of myself. In reality I am still a soi (street) dog and, by now, I am a bit of a loner, surviving on gut instinct and trying hard to remember everything that my Ma had taught me about life.

You might recall that I had been born near to the sea, but I soon discovered that it was easier to find food where large numbers of people lived. Of course, I was not the only dog to realise this and, while more food was available in the larger villages and towns, there were more dogs chasing down that food.

Most of what we ate was human food waste, including packaging when we were desperate. Sometimes we got to eat fresh meat, ie a hunting kill, but as a somewhat shy dog, I tended to miss out on these rare delicacies.

Life as a street dog was brutal. I started most days hungry and thirsty, on edge and somewhat fearful of what lay ahead. Day after day, for three years, this was the pattern of my life and those of all the dogs around me. My own "family" had long since split up and I hadn't seen Ma nor my brothers and sisters since I was a little pup. Sometimes I thought about Ma and hoped that she was well, but my siblings were of no concern to me. In reality they were rivals for food, as was every and any dog I came across.

That said, I was part of a small pack, albeit very much the odd one out in the pack. But being part of a pack gave us "rights" to our own little territory. In the main, the packs all respected each other and we would rarely venture into another pack's territory ... and if we did we could expect a damn good hiding! Sometimes these territories were defined by no more than a road or alleyway with one side belonging to Pack A and the other side belonging to Pack B. As long as we were sensible, healthy and fit, we dogs were generally safe from each other. Humans were our biggest threat. The pack mentality was more for our own protection and, as I have said before, when it came to food, it was every dog for him/her-self.

It didn't help that almost every day we soi dogs would hear dreadful stories about the fates of our fellow hounds.

I remember once a pack of some 15 dogs, living peacefully and happily in and around a temple, were poisoned by local villagers who didn't like dogs. The monks were distraught that such a thing should happen in their temple but, in time, they took in some new dogs. Whether or not these survived I do not know. For we street dogs, the many temples in Thailand are a sanctuary where we are fed and kept safe. That these religious havens, centres of peace and tranquillity, should be so violated is quite abhorrent.

We also heard a story of a group of unwanted puppies who had all been buried alive. Miraculously a rescue party arrived and found one of the puppies just alive. This little pup suffered brain damage (from asphyxiation) but she lived. The humans called her Thora. Little did I know then, that I was to meet Thora later in my life!

And then there is the Trade of Shame, the dog meat trade. Although this is illegal in Thailand, many dogs disappear and we suspect that they are smuggled across the border, through Laos and into Vietnam and then brutally killed for their meat. Sometimes, if I see people moving around at night, I cannot sleep just in case one of them is a dog thief.

The true violence of this street living was brought home to me one night in the most brutal fashion, when I heard terrible screaming coming from an alleyway. So great and so anguished was the cry, that I had to find it and, to my horror, I saw a dog that I recognised with her paw caught in a trap. There was nothing that I nor any of the other dogs that had gathered could do but stare in disbelief.

Just when we thought that things could not get worse, a man came out with a club and beat this dog to death. Thankfully it was all over within a few seconds, and we dogs then ran for our lives as the man turned his anger upon us. Whoever this man was, he hadn't killed for the need to eat ... he had killed for the sake of killing. It was a chilling thought.

I never went near that street again, but I heard that some of the local dogs returned to feast on the carcass of the dead dog. While this might sound revolting to some, I would ask humans who do not understand life on the streets and/or who have never experienced intense hunger, not to judge us dogs. All we are trying to do is survive.

It should be said that all these unimaginable acts of cruelty were matched equally by truly wonderful acts of human kindness. Kind humans feeding us, kind humans protecting us from mean humans and kind humans giving us sanctuary. For us dogs, road accidents were the most common cause of death and injury. Thailand, the country where I lived, had one of the highest fatality rates per head of human population in the world which, in simple terms, meant that they were all crazy drivers ... and this wreaked havoc with us street dogs. Every year far too many of us are killed and/or seriously injured in road accidents, it happens all day and every day.

Maybe this would be a good time to introduce what, at the time, seemed to me to be a somewhat far-fetched urban myth ... a favourite talking point among we soi dogs when resting in the shade. It was rumoured that there was an organisation run by humans that did everything it could to help injured dogs and cats. When I say it was rumoured, what I mean is that we soi dogs repeatedly heard fanciful stories of almost unbelievable human kindness. Of dogs being rescued from human abuse, of dogs being tenderly treated by the roadside after an accident and of dogs being miraculously returned to rude health after receiving terrible injuries. The trouble was, none of these dogs ever re-appeared to tell their tale, so we could not ask them to their snouts whether or not there was any truth to these stories of a dog haven just around the corner.

When I say none of the rescued dogs had ever re-appeared, there was actually one. My Ma told me a remarkable story of a young pup who, we were told, had had both his front legs chopped off by a sword. His crime had been nothing more than to nibble playfully on a pair of shoes; sadly an evil man's shoes. He was just eight months old at the time and couldn't possibly have known better.

So the story goes, two quite wonderful humans from this mythical dog haven (humans who we soi dogs cheekily call St Gill and St John) rescued the pup, nursed him back to health and then made him some false legs. As unlikely as this sounds, a number of dogs that I actually know have seen a real-life dog looking exactly like this pup, wearing athletes' blades, and running like the wind on a local beach. Indeed, one of my dog friends, who rather fancies himself as a linguist, calls this pup "figlio del vento" or "son of the wind".

In retrospect, I cannot believe that so many of us ever doubted that Gill and John Dalley, their pup Cola, and their wonderful dog and cat sanctuary was anything but real. Too many otherwise unexplained miracles were happening all around us; and soon I will tell you more.

But first I must bring you up to date with my own life.

Chapter 9

Heading for disaster

It is 2018 and I am three years old. Somehow I am fit and well and have avoided accidents and injury, minor dog bites aside. Perhaps this is because I had long since decided to fend for myself in towns and villages rather than depend on any individual humans for my safety.

By now I had moved in-land to an old town where there were lots of restaurants serving the farang (tourists). Some of the restaurant owners were kind and would leave food out for us, others didn't like us and felt that stray dogs hanging around their restaurant was bad for trade.

Although permanently hungry, I was fairly settled. I had found a restaurant down a quiet alleyway that left uneaten human food in piles outside its back door. Bizarrely I was living on a menu of burgers, fish, spaghetti, Pad Thai, pizza and food soaked cardboard and paper. Although some of you might think this sounds rather delicious, this food was always mixed up with paper napkins, straws, plastic cups, newspapers, plastic cutlery, floor sweepings and more. But it was food and it was keeping me and the other dogs in our group alive. Of course, we occasionally ate fresh meat such as rats and snakes, but in the main we were eating what humans had started to eat and had been unable to finish.

I suppose I may have become a bit complacent, I don't know. Certainly I had found a safe-ish place to stay with a regular food supply. No one in the alleyway had ever threatened me, indeed they were always quite cheerful saying to us dogs things like "And what would Sir like for dinner today?". I knew this was just a bit of fun and was always grateful for whatever left-overs the humans put out. I think I dropped my guard and, stupidly, I didn't learn every inch of the alleyway that I was living in, as we soi dogs should always do. As a result, I didn't realise that it was a dead end alley, ie only one way in and out. For me, the term dead end was about to take on a horribly sinister double meaning.

12 October 2018

It was a Friday evening and for some reason everyone seemed to be partying. There was certainly more noise than usual and, as it grew dark, we dogs became frightened, as fireworks started to go off. If there's one thing a dog does not like, even a calm dog or a bold alpha dog, it is fireworks. The shriek as they shoot into the sky and the deafening BANG as they explode just terrifies us.

I had heard fireworks from a distance before and that was frightening enough, but I had never experienced them up so close. As a pup I had been told stories of dogs that had literally died of fright and I was very scared indeed.

Then things took a turn for the worse. A group of maybe five or six individuals came into the alleyway, my alleyway, and they were carrying sticks of fire. I have no idea whether or not they meant any harm, but they were shouting and waving fire ... and I lost control of myself and bolted.

Soi Thummasopa is a tiny dead end street in Phuket Old Town. At the top end, near Phuket Road, it has a small hotel (three stars), a furniture / home improvements shop and a motorbike dealer. The rest of the alleyway comprises my little restaurant and a number of derelict buildings.

Where these revellers were going, I don't know, but it seemed to me that they were hunting me down. Even a dog's mind plays strange games at times and I was convinced that they were out to harm me. My fellow dogs all disappeared, mainly into the derelict buildings lining each side of the alleyway. Me? I just ran until, to my horror, I realised that there was nowhere left to go. I was at the end of Soi Thummasopa and, instead of it leading to another street, there was another derelict building blocking my route. In short, there was no way out. Shaking in fear I turned to see the group, probably some 50m away, but still heading towards me. In my mind their chanting was louder and their fires brighter and I knew I was in trouble.

Then, out of the corner of my eye, I saw a tiny gap ... I don't know what it was, it was far too small to be a window, but I ran towards it and jumped in.

I am not sure what happened next. Maybe I banged my head, maybe I passed out, but when I awoke I was in terrible, terrible pain. I could feel sharp objects sticking into my body and I could feel blood oozing out of me. I tried to move and the pain was overwhelming but, worse than that, I realised that I couldn't move however hard I tried.

I was trapped.

Chapter 10

The terror of entrapment

I was trapped. Three simple words, maybe, but an experience that cannot be described in a thousand words.

I realised that, where ever I was, it was no wider than me. It was also very dark, although I could see some shards of light above me. What's more, I was impaled on some object that had cut through my skin and pierced my chest cavity. Breathing was agony, although "agony" doesn't begin to describe the feeling. I was trapped, terrified, in the dark, my body torn open and no obvious way out. That's how it was.

I might only be a dog, but we dogs are survivors, and I was determined to escape. Very carefully I tried to move my paws. Fearsomely sharp pains shot through my body, but I tried again. Wherever I was, whatever I was in, it was made up of sharp objects set into a very rough surround. Every time I moved I felt a new tear in my skin. I knew that I had to move upwards as I was impaled from below, but moving seemed impossible.

The combination of fear and a determination to succeed drove me well beyond any pain threshold that I could ever have imagined. While struggling to gain a few millimetres in height to alleviate my chest pains, I could feel my knees being shredded by the razor sharp surrounds of the area I was trapped in. First one knee, and then the other, ground through to the bone but I didn't stop. I wriggled, I fought away fear and pain and I tried again. At one stage I thought I had some traction on a rear paw and I pushed hard, only for my paw to tear open. I screamed in pain and then tried again. When you are desperate, you fight and fight and, although the pain is overwhelming, somehow your mind overcomes this, albeit only temporarily. More tears, more blood, more pain. To further my predicament, I was becoming thirsty, desperately thirsty, as I was breathing in a lot of dust and my mouth and throat were bone dry.

How long this went on for, I have no idea. I was conscious that sometimes it was dark and at other times there were shafts of light above my hell hole, and I guessed these changes represented days and nights. How many days and how many nights I do not remember, but eventually the pain, the hunger and the thirst began to overwhelm me. Slowly I morphed from frightened to sad. I didn't want to die in this lonely place, but I knew that I was dying and I also knew that there was no way out. By now I was completely drained and dreadfully weak and capable of nothing other than whimpering and crying.

Time passed so slowly, utter helplessness is more than soul destroying, it crushes everything. Even hope, the one thing that I knew I had to cling on to, had long since abandoned me. Thankfully, at last, after enduring so much pain, I could feel peace beginning to envelop me. Strangely it seemed that the pain was subsiding, but in retrospect that would have been me slowly drifting towards the Rainbow Bridge.

Just before crossing the Bridge, before making that final step to forever peace, I vaguely sensed that something had changed. I was utterly wrecked and in a state of near oblivion, but I thought I heard humans shouting.

"There's something there. We think we've found him".

NOTE: *Knight was trapped on the evening of Friday 12 October and he was rescued on the morning of Wednesday 17 October, five nights and four days later. His "hell hole" was a narrow shaft between two derelict buildings. This space was just 430mm wide and, being an internal cavity, was made of rough, unfinished brickwork. Protruding from the brickwork were iron bars of the type used to reinforce building works. It was one of these bars that had sliced open Knight's chest, exposing his rib cage. The gap that Knight had jumped through was nothing more than a large crack, where part of one building was collapsing. It is estimated that he fell over 2m before being impaled on an iron bar.*
A number of locals had reported hearing a dog crying at night. Happily for Knight, after five nights of crying, somone decided to investigate further...

Chapter 11

Rescue. A close encounter with humans

"There's something there. We think we've found him".

17 October 2018

My brain hardly registered the words, in fact I thought I was dreaming, so delirious had I become. Indeed, had I been more conscious, more aware, I might have been frightened of humans so close to me but, by now, I was beyond all state of emotion.

I was vaguely aware of more talk: "How did he get down there? How are we going to get him out? It's too small a gap for us to climb down, not even a child could fit down there!"

The next thing I became aware of was a lot of excited shouting and pieces of brick and building rubble falling on me. Under normal circumstances I would have been pretty unimpressed by this and, although I suppose every piece that hit me must have hurt, I was past caring. I didn't know what was going on, I didn't know that a "rescue operation" was underway and that the humans were creating a big hole in the wall, all I knew was that the Rainbow Bridge was in sight and that my earthly misery would soon be over.

I felt, rather than saw, a snake like object see-sawing over my body. It transpired that this was, in fact, a rope and noose. In time the noose dropped over my head and then pulled tight. Yes, I did panic a bit as, when very tight, it cut off my breathing. While I was blacking out, I was also vaguely aware of upward movement. I could no longer feel the iron bar that had pierced my body and then, suddenly, daylight and lots of cheering. I was in a state of what can only be described as comatose terror; frightened witless but without even the energy to growl ... not even a squeak! Thankfully the terrible tightening around my throat had loosened and I could breathe again, but with that came pain and fear. I was out in the open, free from my hell hole but surrounded by noisy humans. If I had had even a modicum of strength I would have run but, much to my growing terror, I realised that I did not even have the energy to stand up.

Perhaps fearful that I might bite them (at this stage, if a chicken had accidentally run into my mouth, I wouldn't have had the energy to bite it), the humans then dragged me across the building rubble back towards the road. This exacerbated the pain from my many open wounds but, in retrospect, I know that they were helping me. However scared I may have been, I now understand that these humans had rescued me from a painful, lonely death, although it didn't seem like that at the time.

Having dragged me to the roadside, and no doubt still fearful that I might bite them, they then tied my mouth shut with a length of cloth, before carefully lifting me into the back of a pick-up truck.

Thereafter things become a bit of a blur. A short painful journey bouncing about in the back of the truck and then we stopped. I was aware of talking. One man saying "You must help this dog, we have just found him" and another man replying "I am not sure that I can, he is so badly injured". Whatever the outcome, I was lifted out of the pick-up and taken into a building where I was put in a small cage. This transpired to be a local veterinary practice but, other than that ... my memory is vague, I wasn't really aware of my surroundings. The Rainbow Bridge was still beckoning and all I wanted was for my pain and misery to end. I felt a small pin-prick in my front leg and thereafter I don't remember much other than a face looking at me every so often, making tut-tut noises.

Somehow I remained alive ... but only just. A primeval instinct to hang on? I don't really know and what's more, at that point, I was past caring.

October 23rd 2018

After a few days, a man arrived who seemed well respected, as the people listened to what he had to say, and nodded furiously at his every word. He wore a bright orange shirt emblazoned with the words Soi Dog. Strangely this comforted me as I knew that I was a soi (street) dog, although I didn't understand why this human would identify himself a soi dog.

"You must let me take this dog to our hospital" he said "Otherwise he will die".

The vet who had been looking after me absolutely agreed and, it seemed to me, was more than happy to see the back of me! This new man was called Khun Thep and I soon discovered that he worked for an organisation called Soi Dog Foundation, the urban myth of my misguided youth on the streets!

Little did I know, but I had just been found by the only organisation in Asia with both the will and the wherewithal to save my life ...

Chapter 12
Soi Dog Foundation

For the rest of my story to make sense, and to give it credence, I think this would be a good time to tell you about Soi Dog and Gill and John Dalley.

As I am so close to this subject matter (Soi Dog saved my life), I have asked my human to write this chapter for me; so over to you Mr Blue:-

Bringing up my children aside, my time spent volunteering at Soi Dog in Phuket has been by far the happiest time of my life. I first visited in December 2018 (when I met Daengseed) and then again in December 2019 (when I met Knight) and on both occasions I was overwhelmed by the love and care Soi Dog showed to the dogs and cats in its care, as well as to the thousands more on the streets of Phuket and further afield throughout Thailand. Indeed, if Soi Dog "love" could be bottled and sold, the world would be a far better place for it!

Soi Dog Foundation (Soi Dog) was established in 2003 in Phuket, Thailand, by a Dutch national called Margot Homburg and a recently retired English couple, John and Gill Dalley from Yorkshire. These three were deeply disturbed by the state of the dogs and cats they encountered roaming the streets of Phuket and they vowed to help them. Initially they rescued the worst cases and took them to local vets and paid for their care out of their own pockets. Typically these animals would have been hit by cars, attacked by humans (machete wounds being commonplace) and/or they would be suffering from any number of canine afflictions including mange, parvovirus and distemper. Others would quite literally be starving to death, including mums with puppies who could not find enough food to feed themselves let alone their litters.

Realising that the street dog population was out of control, and in conjunction with local vets, Margot, John and Gill set up a sterilisation programme known as CNVR (catch, neuter, vaccinate, return) which does as it says. Dogs and cats were caught, sterilised and vaccinated and then returned to the exact spot where they were found, within 48 hrs maximum, so that they could re-establish themselves in their pack/territory.

At the time, almost 20 years ago now, Phuket had an estimated 70,000 stray dogs alone and the situation was totally out of control. Today the stray dog population is under 6,000 and is now under control. Soi Dog also operates mobile CNVR clinics in Bangkok and across Thailand and has sterilised over half a million dogs and cats at the time of writing.

In September 2004 Gill Dalley was struck down with an extremely rare form of septicaemia which she caught while rescuing a drowning dog from a flooded water buffalo field. At first it was thought that she might die, but happily for the dogs and cats of Asia, she survived, although tragically, it was necessary to amputate both her legs to save her life.

Gill was released from hospital on 22 December and within a week, on 26 December, the coastlines of Southeast Asia were devastated by the infamous tsunami that killed an estimated 200,000 people.

Undaunted, Gill immediately returned to hospital in her wheelchair to help with the rescue operation, counselling the bereaved and seriously injured. This despite losing her best friend in the tsunami; what an extraordinary woman. Her husband John went to Khao Lak, the hardest hit area, where he took on the grim task of sorting, identifying (when possible) and wrapping human remains. An equally extraordinary human being.

The tsunami was headline news around the world for weeks on end and one of the many stories covered by news hacks was the displacement of tens of thousands of cats and dogs. Animal lovers everywhere, including vets and veterinary nurses, offered both cash and hands-on help. As one of the only structured animal rescue services in Asia, Soi Dog became a focal point for this generosity and support.

Although their facilities were extremely limited and the animals needing help almost unlimited, they never wavered. In 2006 Soi Dog was offered a government-owned dog pound in northern Phuket as its base. Lacking in even basic facilities, Soi Dog invested £90K upgrading the shelter and installing a clinic ... only for the government to reclaim their land saying that it was inappropriate for an NGO to run a government owned site.

At around this time, Margot Homburg retired on health grounds. Undeterred, John and Gill found themselves another site in Mai Khao (Northern Phuket) and this time they bought the land ... this site being the home of Soi Dog to this day.

In addition to building a shelter capable of coping with all the dogs and cats needing treatment and/or neutering and/or re-homing, Soi Dog also found itself at the epicentre of many national disasters.

In 2011 there was an outbreak of distemper that affected thousands of dogs, then heavy flooding which displaced thousands more. Thanks to the generosity of Soi Dog supporters, both these potential disasters were contained, and once again Soi Dog proved itself to be a hugely efficient and purposeful organisation.

2011 also saw the launch of the Trade of Shame campaign and

Soi Dog has been at the forefront of the anti-Dog Meat Trade movement ever since. So effective was their campaigning, that the Thai government passed a law banning the killing of dogs and cats for their meat. This act alone has saved the lives of quite literally millions of dogs and cats across Thailand.

In recent years the Mai Khao site has grown to become the largest animal rescue centre in Asia. From 2010 onwards, Gill devoted much of her time to the design of a magnificent dog hospital and in 2014 she laid the first cornerstone. The hospital opened its doors to injured dogs in 2016 and, in 2019, Soi Dog opened an equally impressive hospital for cats. Today this wonderful sanctuary for injured and/or sick dogs and cats houses two animal hospitals (the largest in Asia), an educational centre and a superb visitor centre. As well as this, there are sterilisation units, isolation units, numerous dog runs (designed to house approximately 30 dogs each) and the equivalent for cats!

Tragically Gill was taken by cancer in 2017, aged just 58. After all that she had been through in her life, and all the love and kindness that she had so wilfully given throughout her life, this seemed a particularly cruel fate.

On 29 January 2019 John unveiled a beautiful commemorative statue to his wife Gill. Created by the celebrated Italian sculptor Albano Poli, it is important to record that John paid for this memorial himself. Ask him why and he will simply reply "because Gill would never have forgiven me had I used one penny of Soi Dog funds that could otherwise have been used to help a dog or cat". And so it is that visitors to Soi Dog such as myself, who never had the good fortune to meet Gill, can now see the person whose determination (along with that of John) made possible all that they see around them.

Hundreds of thousands of dogs and cats now lead better lives thanks to the hard working team at Soi Dog and just as importantly, the world at large is learning more of the horrific dog meat trade in Asia.

Soi Dog has rescued more dogs from the dog meat trade than all the better known charities combined, it is now sterilising and treating more stray dogs and cats than any other organisation in the world and it continues to fight the evil dog meat trade, both at government level and by educating the current generation of young Asians.

Soi Dog was created to provide a humane and sustainable solution to managing the stray dog and cat population and to address their dire medical needs. Funding has always come from decent, animal loving individuals around the world who share the vision of Soi Dog and its remarkable founders.

A summary of Soi Dog activities:

CNVR CAMPAIGN

CNVR stands for Catch / Neuter / Vaccinate / Return

Well over 500,000 successful CNVRs resulting in a shrinking dog/cat over-population and the near eradication of rabies on the island of Phuket.

MEDICAL TREATMENT

Providing high quality medical treatment for stray dogs and cats. This has been enormously successful and has mostly eradicated mange (although some cases are inevitable) and rabies in Phuket (only one confirmed case of rabies in recent years).

SHELTERING

Providing shelter and a safe haven for animals that have been the victim of cruelty and abuse, disabled animals, abandoned puppies and those who cannot survive alone on the streets, in addition to the many street dogs and cats that have been injured by cars and motorcycles. (Thailand, as a percentage of population, has one of the highest road accident death rate in the world).

ADOPTION

Finding permanent homes; mainly in the USA, Canada, Europe and the UK; for healthy, loving, homely dogs. The Soi Dog website lists all the dogs available (and suitable) for adoption and there are many partner shelters around the world working to re-home Soi Dogs. With so many beautiful, unwanted dogs in the world, there is no excuse nor need for puppy farms and the like.

www.soidog.org/adopt-a-dog

FIGHTING THE ASIAN DOG MEAT TRADE (DMT)

My Soi Dog Knight will describe the unbelievable cruelty of the DMT elsewhere in this book, but stop to think for a moment. Soi Dog, a privately run animal charity, has achieved a complete ban of DMT in Thailand and has made huge in-roads into Vietnam, South Korea and Cambodia (see Education and Training). Soi Dog is successfully changing the attitude of millions of Asians towards DMT. It is a remarkable achievement.

DISASTER RESPONSE

Everyone knows about the tragic 2004 tsunami, but sadly, natural disasters are a way of life in Asia. There were horrendous killer floods in Bangkok in 2011 and again in Southern Asia in 2016/17. There was an outbreak of usually fatal distemper in 2010 and a rabies scare in north east Thailand in 2018. In all cases, the Soi Dog Emergency Response and Community Outreach teams were the first on the scene to provide food, emergency shelters and evacuation for displaced, threatened dogs and cats.

ERADICATING PUPPY FARMS

In Asian puppy farms, mother dogs are repeatedly impregnated to provide multiple litters a year, usually in squalid conditions. Often mothers die of exhaustion. Pups are removed early, so will not be properly weaned and will not benefit from the natural immunisation process. They are removed early as they look so cute. Often they are then starved, before being caged and taken to markets for sale. These starved puppies are desperate for attention and yelp at every single passer by, thus enhancing their cute-appeal. If the pups are not sold within a week or two, they are simply abandoned in the streets to make way for the next batch. Soi Dog campaigns to shut these farms down while also encouraging the adoption of unwanted puppies and dogs over the purchase of puppies from farms and markets.

ANIMAL WELFARE
Soi Dog was instrumental in the introduction of Thailand's first Animal Welfare Act and also holds a seat on the committee that amends current legislation and recommends additions to it. They also campaign to ensure that these laws are enforced and that sentences are as severe as the new laws allow.

EDUCATION AND TRAINING
Soi Dog funds and operates a training programme to educate young school children, so that they grow up sympathetic to dogs. In addition to a team travelling around schools and villages in Thailand, Soi Dog has recently opened its own Educational Centre at the sanctuary in Phuket. Soi Dog also trains vets from neighbouring countries, so that they can care for dogs and cats back home in their own regions.

If you would like to learn more about Soi Dog, or indeed volunteer at the Sanctuary, please visit their informative website:

www.soidog.org

Chapter 13

Soi Dog heroes

It's me (Knight) again, back at the word pawcessor! As you can imagine, a place such as Soi Dog is full of dogs with quite remarkable stories to tell. Here are just a few of my favourites:-

The most famous Soi Dog of all is Cola, whom I have never met, but all we dogs hold him in awe. You may remember that I mentioned him earlier in my story. When Cola was a puppy (just eight months old), he nibbled on the toe of his human neighbour's shoe. The neighbour went mad and chopped off both his front legs with a ceremonial sword. Poor Cola nearly died, but he was rescued by Soi Dog and, when his stumps were healed, he was fitted with artificial legs. Cola was adopted by John and Gill, co-founders of Soi Dog. Gill was, herself, a double-amputee by this time and it was her prosthetics surgeon who made Cola his new legs. These were later upgraded to Paralympic athlete blades, making Cola the first dog in the world to be fitted with blades. He's our hero; we all called him The Blade Runner.

Search: "Cola. The blade runner dog" on YouTube

Another celebrated Soi Dog is Polo, who is immortalised in Gill Dalley's commemorative statue, as she is the dog that Gill is carrying. When found, Polo's mange and blood parasites were so severe that she was bald and skeletal. Can you imagine skin so itchy and lice infested, that all your hair falls out? I can't. Polo was also suffering from severe malnutrition, organ failure and injuries from human abuse. She was in such a state that it took Gill many months to nurse her back to health personally at her home. Polo, or 'Dame Polo De La Soi' as she prefers to be known, was a favourite of Gill Dalley's and now lives in England with Gill's best friend Donna. As you can imagine, all we Soi Dogs are somewhat in awe of Polo's status in life!

Boonrod, or Uncle Boonrod as all we soi dogs call him, is a legend among dogs. He was stolen from the streets and forced into a small cage along with 11 other dogs, then loaded onto an illegal shipment of some 1000 dogs in three trucks, destined for Vietnam via Laos. This was a dreaded Dog Meat Trade operation and, en-route, the drivers were stopping and brutally killing dogs from the crates, and then cooking them. Thankfully Soi Dog heard of this illegal convoy and, with the help of the Royal Thai Police, were able to intercept all three trucks late one night, while they were waiting to cross the Mekong River into Laos. At the time of interception Boonrod, just a puppy at the time, had been removed from his crate and was lined up for slaughter. Had Soi Dog and the Police arrived just one hour later, Boonrod would not be with us today. He now lives a life of luxury in Italy, adopted by the lovely Paola.

For the record, Soi Dog saved one thousand dogs' lives that night. Just stop and think about that for a minute, ONE THOUSAND dogs lives saved! They gave them all shelter, medical support, food and water. It took a long time but, eventually, all the healthy dogs were found forever homes around the world. Incidentally, one of the dogs rescued was called Miracle and he featured on a British television programme called Britain's Got Talent. He even performed some magic, no wonder he was called Miracle!

There are so many stories that I could tell you, but I must finish this chapter with the story of Gordon. There are many things remarkable about Gordon (not least his bravery and resilience) but I am including him in my story because I met him in the Soi Dog hospital and by chance my (future) human also met him at Soi Dog! Gordon had boiling water poured over his genitals while he slept. All he ever did to deserve this was bark when he wanted attention. His owner then pegged him to the ground and drove a car over his leg to shatter it and then threw him out into the street. Soi Dog rescued him, but had to amputate his leg as it was destroyed. Happily he was adopted by Mel, a Soi Dog employee who, along with Gordon, gave my human a lift to the beach one day long before I even met him!

Oops. I have digressed somewhat in telling my tale, perhaps because the next chapter brings back some terrifying memories, but it is a vitally important part of my story, so here goes ...

Chapter 14
Physical rehabilitation

23 October 2018
It's not looking good. My body is shredded, I am dehydrated and very, very weak and I am terrified of humans. To compound this, Khun Thep has brought me to a place that is absolutely full of humans, they are everywhere I look. Many of them are dressed in orange shirts (more soi dogs?) and some look like farang (tourists). The farang humans all seem to have dogs with them, but these dogs are attached to them by ropes ... I hope they are not going to hurt them.

Khun Thep takes me to a HUGE white building, which I later learn is a hospital. It has a ledger and in this he writes:-

"This dog run to building that no one live there (Soi Thummasopa) at A.Mueang, a dog stuck in wall 4 days, no food or water just cried all time then when local people helped this dog but dog has got big wounds and very weakness that need to treat it asap and after finished cannot send it back as no one know about this dog".

This entry sent shivers down my spine, specifically the bit that said "cannot send it back". Was I going to be trapped in this white building for the rest of my life? Although now, long after the event, I can better structure my thoughts by putting paw to paper, at the time I was in no state to ponder my future. I was wracked with pain and just wanted peace, however or wherever it came from.

Dr Bow was the first of eleven vets in total to care for me during my time at Soi Dog. She clearly understood the pain that I was in and was very, very gentle with me.

Her entry log reads:-
Arrived at SDF on October 23rd 2018, brought in by animal rescue officer Khun Thep from the local vet where he was taken six days prior by local people who found the dog stuck in a wall of an abandoned building (4 days with no food and no water). Local people did not know where this dog came from.

Dr Bow went on to say:-
Treatment Notes
23.10.2018 - Admitted to intensive care. Dehydrated, depressed, skinny, weak and very scared (not willing to walk, but can stand), abrasion wounds over the whole body especially the thorax, hind limbs and paw. Bloodwork: anaemic and E canis infection. Was sedated, wounds cleaned, disinfected, using Manuka honey and wounds dressed. Put on E canis treatment, supplements, pain relief and IV fluids. Wound dressing daily.

Intensive care meant a small cage, but roomy enough to stand and turn around. When I first tried to do this I noticed that I had tubes attached to my body. Whatever they were doing, I do not know, but over the next few days I started to feel better, although the fear, intense fear, never left me. I started to eat and drink and this gave me strength. I was still very scared, but it seemed to me that my wounds were healing well, although still extremely painful.

Dr Bow and other vets visited me 2-3 times every day and they seemed happy with my progress. Sometimes, when they took me out of my cage I was so frightened that I soiled myself, but they never scolded me. A few days after I was admitted, I overheard someone say: "Some of these wounds worry me. I think he will need surgery in the near future once the infection is under control and his bloodwork improves. His hind limbs seem very lame, probably due to wounds healing incorrectly, probably overgranulation".

On 29 November, a full month after I had been admitted, I was deemed strong enough for reconstructive surgery. Happily I had no idea what this meant, so I didn't have the chance to worry. All I remember is ... well nothing really. One minute I was awake and shaking with fear as someone removed me from my cage; and then I was awake again, back in my cage and all bandaged up and in more pain than I had been for a while. I must have cried out as someone adjusted a button on my tubes and I slipped into a deep, deep sleep. When I woke there were a number of smiling faces peering at me. "You won't understand this" said Dr Eed who had performed some remarkable surgery, "But the good news is that you will be able to walk again although, perhaps, you will not be able to run very fast!".

The next few days passed in a blur. I am not sure what was in the tubes attached to me, but sometimes, I am sure I felt myself flying. I imagined myself as a cross between a soi dog, a pegasus and an eagle, gliding through the sky and barking at all those little humans down on the ground below me! More importantly, I was feeling stronger by the hour and some (very small) degree of hope was beginning to return.

It was not all good news though. For some unfathomable reason, someone had stuck a lampshade on my head, which meant that I couldn't lick my balls, as we dogs like to do on a regular basis. To make matters worse, when eventually they removed the lampshade, I noticed that my balls were missing. Yes, they had gone! Honestly, as if I didn't have enough problems to deal with already! This really was a BIG shock as we dogs like a good lick down there, it's what we do when there's nothing else to do. If I'm honest, I'm not sure what purpose my balls ever served, but I knew I was going to miss them ... indeed I already did.

Later, on that same day of discovery, I may even have growled slightly at the nurse who was caring for me, which would have been a bit unfair as I doubt she nicked them! Actually I remember her very well; she was called Sarah and there are two reasons that I remember her. Firstly, she always wore a Micky Mouse badge and people called her Disney Sarah and secondly (although of course I didn't know this at the time), she knew my human (to be) and discussed my case with him in December 2018. Of course he didn't know me either as I was in hospital, but I like to believe that fate was already aligning our stars.

Before changing my dressings, Disney Sarah always looked at a clipboard on an adjacent wall and, one day soon after surgery, she left this on a work surface next to my cage. Being a curious fellow, I decided to take a quick look at it and this is what it said:-

29 November 2018
Removed all fistulas on the left side of body, repaired right knee wound and rebuilt 4th digit on the right hind paw. Continue with wound dressing, antibiotics and pain relief, plus anti-inflammatories and blood supplements.

A few days after this operation, I was taken out of intensive care and given a new place to live. My new den comprised two rooms connected by a hatch. One room was indoors and the other was open to the elements, albeit caged with bars so that I couldn't run away ... not that I was in any state to run! I soon discovered that the Soi Dog "dog" hospital had 44 such "wards" as well as a reception area, an intake room, two isolation wards, various assessment rooms, two operating theatres, an intensive care unit, a laboratory for blood and skin analysis, a hydrotherapy room, a physio centre and even a grooming room. Even in my poor state, I was mightily impressed with what was around me!

When I was alone in my rooms I felt peaceful. Although there was a lot of dog barking, the ambient sound was soothing music as the hospital piped classical music into every room. How ironic that humans should play us Bach to stop us barking! This certainly helped me relax and I also discovered that the air conditioning unit passed air through various UV filters which killed off any germs. Many human hospitals don't have these facilities and I was beginning to understand that I was in good hands, however frightening I found the whole experience.

On 07 January 2019, my notes read:-
Good appetite, bloodwork very good, all wounds healed. Ready to move to shelter run and start work with Behaviour Team, as very timid and shy.

Ten weeks after I had been admitted to the Soi Dog hospital, I was deemed well enough to move on and make way, within the hospital, for another injured dog. By now I had acquired the name Knight, apparently as I had been very stoic throughout my treatment, resulting in one of the nurses saying: "He's such a brave knight, we should call him Knight".

In just three months I had morphed from just one of 600,000,000 street dogs roaming the planet, through being a grievously injured dog, to a patient in perhaps the most advanced dog hospital in the world, and then on to being a dog with a name of my own, Knight, albeit still a very damaged dog.

But my biggest challenge was yet to come.

Clockwise from above:
- I was born on Phuket Island, somewhere near Phuket town
- Young, free and healthy
- Looking for food
- We are called street dogs for a reason!
- Once we were wolves

Soi Thummasopa,
Phuket Island

Cutting an access
hole to rescue me

You can just see
me in the cavity

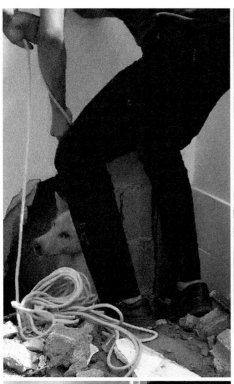

"I felt, rather than saw, a snake like object see-sawing over my body"

Back out in the open for the first time in days... and more terrified than you could ever imagine

The intensive care unit...
my home for three weeks

Humane Education Centre, the
most important classroom in Asia

The magnificent Soi Dog dog
hospital, designed by Gill Dalley

Young Asian children learn about dogs and cats

Love Lake... Mr Blue and I walked around here a hundred times!

One of my chums having a check-over

Soi Dog's Walk of Love: Kimba and
Soi Daengseed share a memorial star

The wonderful
Visitor Centre

Working out in the
hydrotherapy pool

จิลล์ ดัลลีย์
ผู้ร่วมก่อตั้งมูลนิธิเพื่อสุนัขในซอย
จากวันที่ 29 มกราคม 2502 ถึงวันที่ 13 กุมภาพันธ์ 2560

John Dalley, a co-founder of Soi Dog, in front of the beautiful memorial to his beloved wife Gill. We dogs call them St John and St Gill and we all owe them so much. With tripod Soi Chiro

Losing her legs didn't stop St Gill from working around the clock

John Dalley's favourite photo of Gill

Gill meets Cola, a match made in heaven

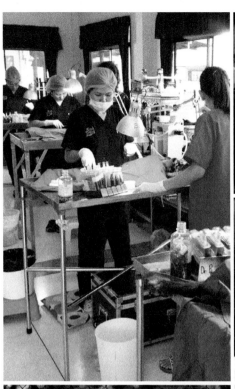

Soi Dog vets at work

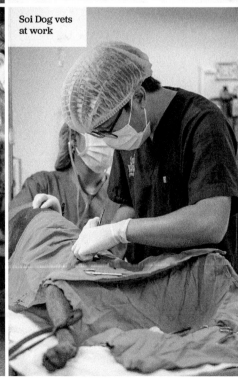

SOI DOG HEROES

Cola The Blade Runner.
I have never met Cola but my human has

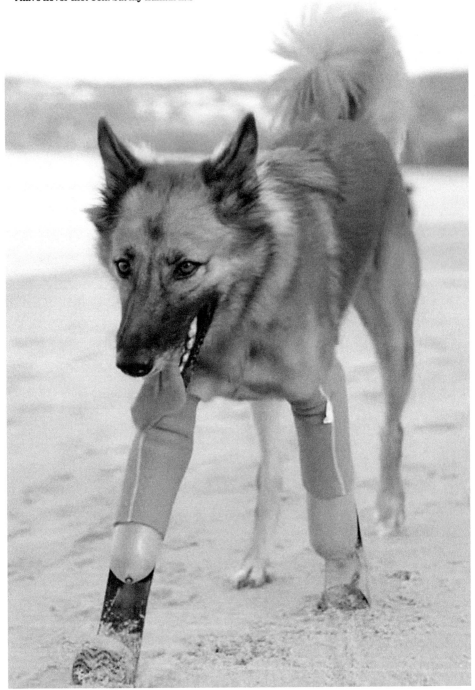

St Gill with Polo on the day she was rescued

Polo now!

Boonrod, saved from the vile dog meat trade

Gordon and Mel gave my human a lift to the beach in this jalopy

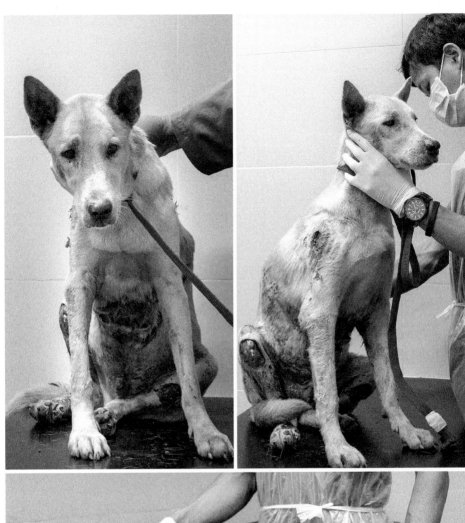

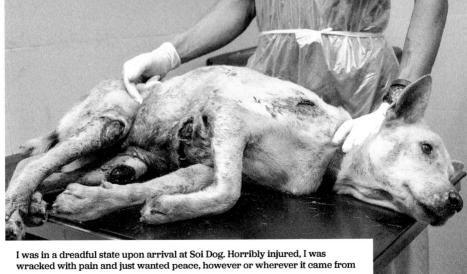

I was in a dreadful state upon arrival at Soi Dog. Horribly injured, I was wracked with pain and just wanted peace, however or wherever it came from

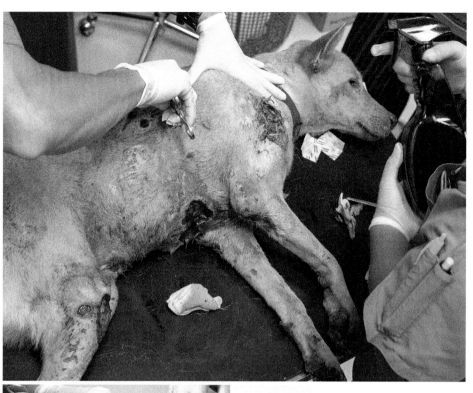

The vets and nurses start work, cleaning and disinfecting my wounds. My thorax was torn open and my hind legs were shredded. Many hands make dog work!

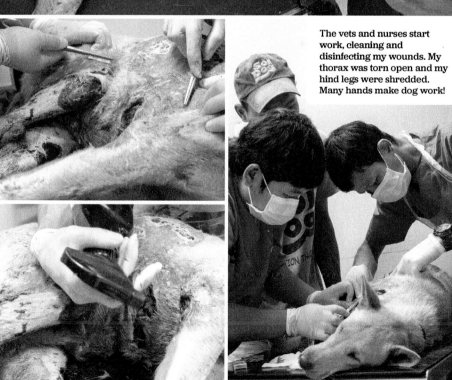

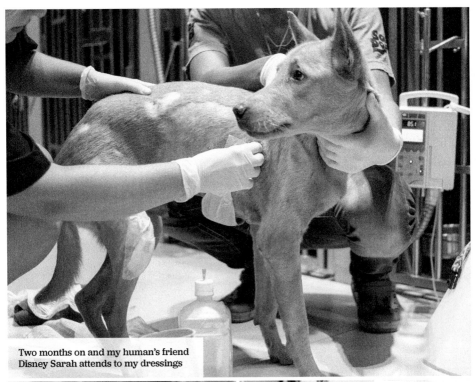

Two months on and my human's friend Disney Sarah attends to my dressings

My wounds are healing, although I am still a mess

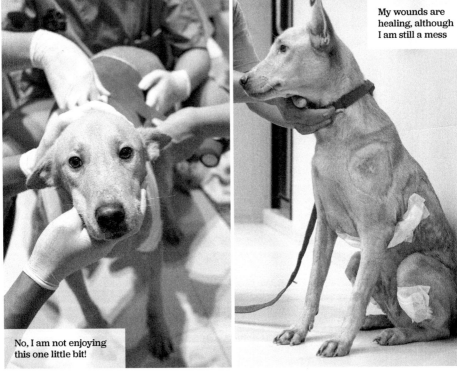

No, I am not enjoying this one little bit!

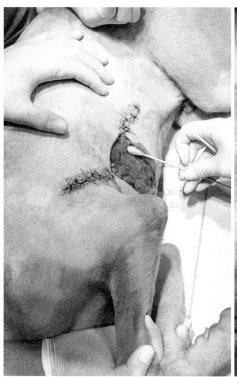

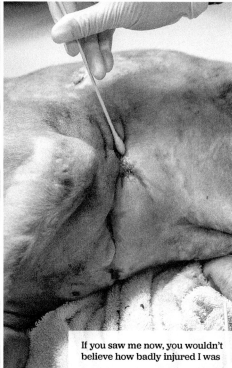

If you saw me now, you wouldn't believe how badly injured I was

Being taught deportment by one of the many Soi Dog angels

Relaxing in my own private suite

Curtis. Without his patience, care and love, I would still be hiding in the corner of a run, shaking with fear

My dear friend Daengseed ❤

Clockwise from top left:

Beautiful Bravoo, amazing Aylin
and fearless Fendi. Fendi is in
one of those horror cages...

Bath time in A3.
That's me on the bench

My human with
Daengseed in 2018

Khun Doe, the undisputed
boss of our run

Full Run, No restriction, Off-leash area avalible

My Top Trump card

Knight -- A3

A bit shy and nerverse when outside the run. Will take sometime to build the trust. Be patient. Walk well.

Male   *Date of Birth:* 08-10-2015

Kat before she broke her wrist

Mr O!

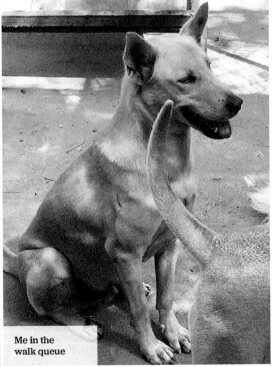

Me in the walk queue

The greatness of a nation and its
moral progress can be judged by
the way its animals are treated.

Mahatma Gandhi

Chapter 15

My friend Curtis

It seems only natural to me now that this chapter should be entitled "My friend Curtis" but when I first met Curtis, I pooed and wet myself in fear.

It really is hard to put into pawspective how frightened I was. You have to remember that I was a soi/street dog, so feral and totally unused to humans in close proximity. And yet here I was, just discharged from almost three months in hospital where, almost every day, I had been washed, prodded, medicated and stitched up (literally) by humans. To achieve all of the above, it took one human (sometimes two) to hold me still, while another human performed whatever had to be done. I never got used to this, it terrified me every time, not least as what they were doing was often painful, even though it was necessary to make me better.

Back to Curtis. I soon discovered that he led the behavioural team at Soi Dog. He has many years of experience working with timid dogs, although I was probably one of his biggest challenges! He leads a team of five behaviourists including himself and they work from what are called the C runs, special enclosures for we "difficult" dogs.

Upon leaving the hospital, I was moved to C3. C3 could best be described as a large kennel, maybe 5m by 3m, with a concrete floor and blockwork walls. Being scared witless, I was very relieved to discover, upon arrival, that I didn't have to share this larger den with any other dog; I had it all to myself. Despite its ample size, I squeezed myself as deep into one corner as possible and just shook and shook and shook.

Eventually exhaustion took over and, at some stage, I must have fallen asleep. I awoke to the smell of chicken very close to my nose and when I opened my eyes, I saw a man. He was outside the cage, sitting very still on the ground and looking in, but not looking directly at me. I immediately soiled myself, it scared me so much. I had got used to the faces, voices and smells of those people in the hospital and, although this man wasn't anywhere near me, he was new and that frightened me. Happily he realised this, slowly got up and walked away. My eyes followed him until he disappeared around a corner and then I remembered the chicken. Three pieces all for me, they were delicious!

The next day this man returned and, again, made no effort to approach me. Indeed, it seemed to me that he didn't even notice me, although he did hang around my kennel for quite some time, before depositing more chicken and wandering off. This man, as you will have guessed, was Curtis and he really, really spooked me … for no reason other than I was in a terrible state and scared of everything around me!

At this stage, I think it might be worth reviewing Curtis' own notes about me, to see what HE was thinking:-

Curtis on Knight - January 2019

At first, he was completely shut down. He would generally show no response if you went towards his kennel, but stayed outside. If you went in he would become terrified, and would shake and often soil himself. He would watch you, and sometimes look as if he wanted to run away, but would mostly just press himself against the wall, and try to disappear into the corner.

I think this pattern continued for a week or two. Curtis would visit me every day, sometimes twice a day and he would speak quietly to me, while at the same time offering tasty morsels to tempt me to approach him. Although he is a big, strong man, Curtis had a very gentle voice and, as I was soon to discover, an even gentler touch. After a while, and much to my surprise, I found that I was not so scared of him ... as long as he kept his distance. Then one day, after a month or so, and quite unexpectedly, I felt an almost involuntary quiver in my tail when Curtis approached for his daily visit. Wow, I was wagging my tail at a human!

Curtis on Knight - February 2019
The first signs he showed that he was starting to feel some sort of positive emotion was that his tail would wag. At first, it was very brief, just like a twitch, that stopped as soon as it started. It would happen as I approached but that was it. He would also sometimes make soft eye contact, rather than averting his eyes.

Until now I had been tensing up whenever Curtis came my way, pressing myself into the wall as if to disappear within it. But now I found myself allowing him to come closer and closer without tensing. I am not sure if I was just getting used to him, or whether I was beginning to understand that he wasn't going to hurt me, but I certainly found that I could stay relatively calm, even when he entered my little den.

Curtis on Knight - mid February 2019
He now allows me to touch him gently. Initially he did not show much of a response. He did not seek attention, but would allow touch. A short period of time after this, he would then accept the touch, and seemingly enjoy it, resting his head down gently while being petted. At this early point, the only signs that he was enjoying things were that he was calm and not tense, and that he would still sometimes wag his tail very briefly when being approached.

Much to my surprise, I now found myself excited by Curtis' visits. When he entered my den I found myself approaching him, then usually losing my nerve and heading back towards my corner. This went on for quite a while. I wanted to say "hello" and deep down I knew that he wasn't going to hurt me, but I didn't quite have the courage or confidence to walk up to him. I should say here that Curtis was remarkably patient and never, even once, did he force the issue. One day we were sitting in my corner opposite each other and I found myself leaning towards him. Very slowly; very, very slowly, Curtis moved his hand over me and very gently stroked me. I tensed automatically and could feel his hand lifting, then I realised that I wasn't scared and I started to relax. Indeed, I found this new sensation of Curtis touching me very soothing and quite reassuring. "I think we may have just turned a corner, sweet Knight"; Curtis whispered in my ear and I felt my tail wagging in response.

Curtis on Knight - mid April 2019

One day, as I approached, instead of walking halfway toward me then moving away, he ran right up to the kennel gate, with his tail wagging fully. When I went in, he moved back to his spot in the back corner, and stayed there. Over the next few days he repeated this greeting, approaching with a wagging tail. Soon he started to continue wagging his tail when I petted him in the corner, and he was now clearly enjoying the contact. This was such a special time for me as I realised that he was beginning to trust me.

This was a very strange time for me as I was making friends with a human! I had spent most of my life avoiding humans and certainly not trusting them and now I liked one. Actually, I more than liked him, Curtis was becoming the focus of my life. He had been visiting me every day for weeks, sometime twice a day, and just seeing him, even when he was passing by without stopping, made my heart beat a little bit faster.

I had noticed that Curtis often walked past my den with another dog attached to him by a rope and this had intrigued me, as this is what I had seen with the farang (tourists) when I was first brought into Soi Dog. Which is why I felt a mix of excitement and trepidation when, one day, Curtis arrived in my den with one of these ropes.

Curtis on Knight - late April 2019

Eventually it was possible to put a lead on him and take him out of his kennel. He was nervous at first so we went for very short sessions outside. It was clear that he was very keen to go outside, now and every day, when I turned up. He would run up to the gate, tail wagging; very excited and keen to go out. He would head out with full enthusiasm, but was extremely nervous in this new environment and/or when he saw new people. He would then want to head back to safety. He wagged his tail and turned to look at me when something scary happened, and we would calmly head back to his kennel. If he was really scared, I would pick him up, and he would be calm in my arms, happy to be carried past whatever it was that had frightened him.

Interestingly, when I had walked past his kennel with other dogs in the early days, he would sometimes tentatively approach them with a wagging tail, even when he was still scared of me. Once he was no longer scared of me, he took every opportunity to approach other dogs who went past, sniffing them and showing interest. It was clear to me that he was quite comfortable with dogs.

May 2019

I've moved to a new kennel which I really like as it is in a quieter spot, with fewer strange people wandering around. There is an area directly outside that is like a yard which I can walk around without encountering strangers or things that would scare me, like cars and delivery vans. I am walking on a lead every day with Curtis and it is such fun ... I really cannot believe how much I like this human.

He reminds me of my Ma, always there to look after me and to keep me safe. I now find my walks very relaxing and I even stop to sniff and sometimes to roll in the grass, it is such fun! I am still scared of everyone other than Curtis, but he is encouraging me to explore areas that previously scared me and he is beginning to introduce me to his friends. "Don't be afraid, sweet Knight, these people are my friends" he would tell me in his gentle and calming voice; and I found myself believing him and trusting his every word. Interestingly, his friends all wear the same shirt that he does. I have noticed that they all have the word "Behaviourist" on their chests.

Curtis on Knight

He soon became relaxed on his walks, and then it was a case of slowly taking him to other areas. Now that he had learned that walking could be fun, he was able to walk in areas of the shelter that he had been too afraid to go to before. He also became more trusting in general, because the people that he now encountered out with their dogs were much less scary than the types he had met previously. I also introduced him to more people and other team members. Also shelter staff got to interact with him and join us on walks or walk with him. As he seemed to like other dogs, he was also able to enjoy seeing them. He would sometimes stand and watch other dogs in the off-lead area as they were running around and playing. When he got the chance he would approach and wag his tail at some of them through the fence.

July 2019

I've moved again and this time I am in a run with other dogs! Curtis tells me that they are all "special needs" dogs, mostly very shy like me. As a result, I do not find them particularly intimidating, although I cannot help being nervous in my new surroundings. It is such fun to be with other dogs again, especially as they are all so gentle, but I am not seeing much of Curtis and this makes me sad as I miss him so much. I often see him walk by with other dogs and

I try and catch his attention but I am not always successful. When he does visit me, I get very excited and he tells me that I am doing really well. He has explained that I have to become independent of him as it is an important part of my development, but I'm not sure that I want to develop if it means not being with Curtis.

August 2019

One day, much to my surprise, I was taken back to the hospital. Although I had healed wonderfully since my entrapment, I was still walking with a limp and my back legs felt very stiff. Curtis had said that I was now brave enough for further treatment and he was right. Although still scared, I wasn't terrified and I was able to control myself, although not my shivers!

It had been decided that I needed twice weekly sessions of laser therapy and physiotherapy (massage) to help relax my thigh muscles. After a while I found this process very relaxing and I even started to enjoy it! Four months of quite intense physiotherapy (they worked me hard!) resulted in a better gait and more comfort (less squat). I was really pleased with this as I had been struggling a bit with my walking but hadn't wanted to say anything in case it upset Curtis. Now I could walk pain-free, as long as I didn't over do things. Okay, I was never going to run like I used to, but I was quite mobile and for that I was truly grateful.

Curtis on Knight - September 2019

By now Knight was much more confident in general. He was more comfortable walking and noticeably more relaxed with the things he encountered at the shelter. This is when he got to know more people, and joined a group of dogs. He was initially nervous in his new surroundings, and would stand up at the fence, jump around and wag his tail like helicopter, whining whenever he saw me. This is when I deliberately distanced myself because, in time, we are hoping that he will be adopted into a family environment so it is important that he learns to socialise with as many people as possible.

Sub-note from Curtis

This is the most painful part of my job, saying goodbye. I had come to love Knight and in my mind he was nothing short of a miracle dog. I missed him every day and I still do, but he had to learn to live and enjoy life without me.

I often think of Knight and he will always be in my heart. He was a huge challenge and there were times when I feared that he might have been beyond help, but he had the will to live and he was a fighter. I just know that he has a wonderful life ahead of him.

Chapter 16

My friend Daengseed

One day, in October 2019, Curtis said to me "I think you are ready to go and live in a full run with more dogs now". He said this with a huge grin on his face and it seemed to me, a little tear in his eye. Without Curtis I do not think I would now be alive or, if I was, I am not sure that my life would be worth living. He is the most caring human I have ever met. So, while the idea of possibly making new friends was exciting, the thought of losing Curtis was devastating. I tried to convey this to him but he seemed so excited on my behalf that his enthusiasm started to rub off on me.

While I had been in the Soi Dog hospital I had enjoyed what you humans would call a private room. I understand that two-legs pay a lot of money for this while being repaired, but at Soi Dog, it is offered to us as standard. At the time, I was in considerable pain and very distressed so I probably didn't appreciate how lucky I was. A private room, specialist surgeons, nurses checking in on me all day and every day, gentle music in the background, canine physio, hydrotherapy, massage, healthy meals and a little bit of exercise as and when I was ready for it. Believe you me, the very best of Obama Care and Nuffield Hospitals have nothing on Soi Dog!

After my spell in the hospital, I had spent quite a long time in a single kennel which I didn't much like. At the time I was too scared to go into a dog run but Curtis visited me every day, and sometimes the lovely Eve or Khun O (aka Mr O!), or one of the other Behaviourists, so each and every day had its highlights.

However now it was time for me to move on and go and live in a "run" of many dogs. Let me explain. At any one time, Soi Dog accommodates up to 800 dogs. All these dogs have been rescued from one thing or another. Some are young, some are old, some are super confident and brave, others like me are not so sure; a bit overwhelmed by all that is going on around them. When they arrive at Soi Dog they are repaired and when ready, allocated to a run. There are many different runs, starting with the Puppy Run and progressing though life to the OAP Run (OAP, I later discovered, is an English abbreviation of Old Age Pensioner). There are runs for confident dogs, shy dogs, overly boisterous dogs, dogs rescued from the abhorrent dog meat trade and more.

Curtis decided that I should go to live in A3, which is a run of 30 healthy dogs, give or take one or two on any day. Some were tripods, some were shy and some were a bit boisterous and noisy for my liking. Indeed we were a mixed bag, to use a human expression.

To be honest I was quite frightened. The last time I had been this close to so many dogs was 12 months ago when I was on the streets. At the time I was fit and streetwise. Now, after 12 months of human care, I knew that I couldn't fend for myself. I couldn't hunt and catch a squirrel (Thailand's Finlayson squirrels are a delicacy among we dogs!) or even grab a left over pizza before anyone else spotted it. Also, thanks to my damaged legs, I couldn't fight for and protect my food as I had done in the past. It was a strange feeling. By nature I wanted to escape my cage and my controlling leash, but logic told me that I wouldn't survive more than a week or two back on the streets, if that.

So, in August 2019, almost a year after my rescue, I moved into A3!

Wow, was that a shock to the system. Almost immediately I came face to face with Juturna, an absolutely magnificent and extremely handsome tripod who was the alpha of A3, the undisputed top dog. Juturna looked me in the eye, growled just enough to catch my undivided attention, and said "Welcome to A3 kid. I'm the boss around here despite what Aylin might tell you. Keep out of my way, don't cross my path and keep your nose clean and you'll be okay. Challenge me on anything ... and you'll regret it!".

Boy, was I on edge!

By chance, the very next dog I met was Aylin. At first I wasn't sure whether Aylin was actually a dog or a lion, so extraordinary was her mane. Aylin smiled at me. "So you've met Juturna" she said. "He's a bit of a ballsy boy and rather fancies himself, so we let him think that he's our alpha. This time last year, I was the alpha, along with my friend Lamia. We made a great team and all the dogs respected us; I was the brains and Lamia was the beefcake, although truth told, Lamia was a bit of a softie, but none of the dogs had the courage to challenge her. Steer clear of Juturna, he can be a bit aggressive at times and don't, under any circumstance, underestimate me. I've seen dogs come and go in this run. I've been alpha and, every now and again, I've taken a back seat ... but I am still here and all those fancy wonder boys have moved on. Make no mistake, I am the real boss of A3". This was all said in a quiet but steely voice ... Aylin was certainly hugely impressive!

Phew, what was I to make of all this? The magnificent Juturna strutting around like an alpha, the equally glorious Aylin reminding me that things weren't always as they seemed, and 27 other dogs looking at me and no doubt thinking; Who is this and where does he fit in to our pack?

And then something remarkable happened. I had carefully manoeuvred myself into a quiet corner at the back of the run and was taking a breather and wondering what in the world to do next when I heard a gentle "Hello Knight". I looked up I found myself face to face with yet another dog. Oh no, I thought, not another wannabe alpha, but this dog was different. She was creamy brown, not dissimilar to me but with a curly tail, she had a beautiful face and one lopsided ear. Like me, she was covered in scars although, perhaps, not quite as many. "Hello" she said again, "My name is Daengseed which, as you probably know, means 'wobbly legs' in Thai. I see that your legs are a bit wobbly too. How are you settling in?". And so started the best four-legs friendship of my life.

Daengseed was a little older than me and she had had a really rough time. She had been involved in a road accident and a couple of dog fights, which had left her with open wounds. These wounds had become infected and maggots had set in. Her flesh was literally rotting upon her, it must have been agony, poor thing. Some well intentioned human had picked her up and taken her to the Phuket Government Dog Pound for care. Sadly the Government Dog Pound (or GDP as we dogs call it) is no Soi Dog haven. For starters the runs are huge, meaning that dogs of all sizes and conditions are mixed together, resulting in multiple dog fights, some fatal. Add to this, there are no medical facilities and no employed carers (other than feeders), although kind farang volunteers turn up most days to help clean the runs and befriend the dogs. All of which begs the question: What is the purpose of the GDP? To my mind and to that of Daengseed, it is there simply because there has to be somewhere on the island for people to dispose of unwanted dogs. Likewise there has to be somewhere for local officials to "lock up" dogs that have been reported as being vicious or whatever. The sad thing is, and I've heard this from many dogs, you only have to bark at a mean human and you can be locked up for life. Being a street dog in Asia is not easy.

Back to Daengseed. She was utterly terrified in the GDP. She was weak from her wounds and getting weaker by the day as she was getting no food - feeding is a free for all in the GDP. The fit get fitter, the weak fall by the wayside. Happily Soi Dog sends a vet up to the GDP every week to help out. The Government doesn't pay for this service; Soi Dog does it for the love of dogs.

When Dr Su saw Daengseed, she was horrified and immediately took her over to the Soi Dog hospital for emergency treatment. In time my new friend was signed off as fit, and re-homed in A3, limp and all. Fortunately for her, it was during a period of Aylin and Lamia leadership, and they were very supportive. In time Daengseed's confidence grew and her legs grew stronger, although they always clicked together as she walked.

Daengseed told me how the runs worked. "All the A and B runs are managed by a kind human called Khun Doe" she explained. "Whatever Juturna and Aylin might have told you, Khun Doe is our real alpha and we all do what she tells us. Not only because we are slightly scared of her, but because she really cares for us. In the same way that some of our humans are scared of the man they call God or Buddha or Muhammad, but love and revere this person, we are the same with Khun Doe. Don't misunderstand me" she continued, "Khun Doe is not our God but she is our guardian angel, so make friends with her as soon as you can".

As the day wore on Daengseed told me more and more about A3 and I began to realise, not for the first time, how lucky I was. We had a walk every day with humans called volunteers, we had one good meal a day and we had a bath every week. If anything was wrong with us we received medical care that same day and if it was serious, we would be taken to the Soi Dog hospital. Khun Doe and her team were on hand all day to keep an eye on us and to keep our runs clean and we even had night staff in case we ran into problems while the world slept. Yes, I would have preferred to have been a free agent on the streets, but here I was safe and I had a new four-legged friend that I knew I could trust.

That night I slept close to Daengseed on the second shelf of her sala. I didn't sleep that well and I had my recurring nightmare about being trapped in a house, but this time the house was on fire. At some stage I must have yelped as I heard Daengseed whisper "It's alright Knight, you're quite safe now. Think about your future and sleep peacefully my dear new friend". The nightmare subsided and exhaustion took over.

The next day Daengseed said "I want you to meet two very special friends of mine". I wasn't sure that I was ready to make new friends just yet and must have said as much, but Daengseed assured me that all would be okay. "I won't be here for ever" she said, "and you need to know who else you can trust". I didn't really think much about this comment at the time, so off we went to socialise.

"This is Bravoo" said Daengseed and I found myself staring at a jet black dog with the most beautiful deep brown eyes that I have ever seen. I was mesmerised and felt quite naked, almost as if Bravoo's eyes were looking right through me and into my soul. "Hello" said Bravoo, his tail wagging gently from side to side, "and welcome to A3. I saw you yesterday and wanted to say Hello then, but you looked somewhat overwhelmed, so I thought it best to leave you chatting with Daengseed. How are you settling in?". I was just about to answer when I sensed a sniff behind me, or rather a sniff of my behind! "Hi" said a little black and white dog, "You smell okay! I'm Fendi, by the way, although some of the humans call me Houdini as I'm always trying to escape". These were Daengseed's special friends and they both welcomed me as one might welcome a family member.

"Your reputation precedes you" said Bravoo. "We've all heard so much about you" said Fendi. "Is it true you were stuck in a building for weeks?" asked Bravoo; "without food and water?" added Fendi. For the first time in a long time I found myself relaxing. It seemed that the story of my rescue, repair and rehabilitation had swept through the runs, albeit in typically exaggerated form.

"Yes" confirmed Daengseed, "We have heard all sorts of stories about you by listening in to the Behaviourists; and we are all so pleased to meet you at last."

"So that's how you knew my name!" I exclaimed to Daengseed. I hadn't even been in A3 for 24 hours and already I had three wonderful, caring new friends.

That afternoon I asked Bravoo and Fendi about their lives. Bravoo, being the gentleman he was, harrumphed and tried to change the subject. I thought this rather strange until I noticed that little Fendi had gone very pale and was noticeably trembling from her ears down to her paws.

"I am sorry, have I said something wrong?" I asked, as I hadn't meant to upset anyone.

"That's alright" said Fendi, "You weren't to know" and then, very quietly, she told me her story:-

Fendi had started life much like me. She lived near a small village on mainland Thailand and survived on a combination of wildlife kills, human food waste and the occasional kind human putting out food for the local soi/street dogs.

One evening a man came towards her with fresh meat in his hand. Just as she was about to gratefully receive it, he smashed her over the head with something very hard and then, before she could recover, he noosed her with rope, tied up her muzzle and literally threw her into the back of a nearby van. The van was full of other dogs, all in a similar predicament.

The van drove to a yard where Fendi saw literally hundreds of dogs packed in tiny cages with limbs sticking out in all directions, some clearly broken. Indeed some of the dogs seemed to be already dead. Within minutes Fendi was forced into a similar cage and this cage was then loaded onto a large truck. Fendi thought that there were three such trucks, with probably 30 crates stacked on each of the vehicles.

Then started the most horrific three days of her life as the trucks drove along very bumpy roads in intense heat. None of the dogs were given food or water and many of the dogs in the lower cages died of a combination of injuries and heat related asphyxia ... the cages in the middle of the trucks had no air and were surrounded by dogs in other cages. With every bump of the road, dogs howled in distress and pain.

After three days, the trucks arrived at the Mekong River, in Nakhon Phanom province. On the other side of the river was Laos and thereafter Vietnam, a country which happens to sustain the most brutal and inhuman aspects of the dog meat trade.

Needless to say Fendi was sick with terror ... all us pups had been told about the dog meat trade and its brutality. We had also been told that, although the dog meat trade was illegal in Thailand, there were many evil humans who captured dogs and smuggled them over the Thai border into Laos.

Suddenly a new noise took over, the wailing of sirens. Fendi told me that she didn't really understand at the time what was happening but this is what she later discovered. Our saviours at Soi Dog had spotted the illegal shipment and, with the help of the Royal Thai Police, had intercepted the trucks just before they crossed the river. All the crates were gently unloaded and laid on the ground under loose covers to keep off the beating sun. Although it took forever, or so it seemed to Fendi, all the dogs were removed from their death crates and, in time, taken to Soi Dog's shelters for evaluation and care.

"In all, Soi Dog saved over 1000 dogs that day" said Fendi, still trembling. "I don't usually talk about it but we like you Knight, you are special".

The telling of this story had drained Fendi and, as you can imagine, I felt very humbled. That evening we all slept close to each other in our sala. I had got myself in a mess in the house, but Fendi had been to hell and back and had survived, just like my Uncle Boonrod.

Weeks passed by and I got to know all the other A3 dogs. In the main they were a good pack, although I was quite wary of the more noisy among them. I tended to keep myself to myself when things got loud, although to be fair, I never felt threatened. Even Juturna left me alone; but then again I had Daengseed, Bravoo and Fendi looking after my back.

I spent most of my time with Daengseed who, every now and again, would disappear for a day or two without explanation. After my faux-pas with Fendi, I decided it would be best not to ask anything but, much to my distress, Daengseed seemed to be ageing faster than the rest of us.

One day, after a hugely threatening and somewhat foreboding storm that frightened us all, Daengseed confided in me. Her kidneys were failing and her time on this earth was very nearly over. I was devastated, but Daengseed seemed very composed, explaining that she had been receiving life-extending treatment at the Soi Dog hospital for months. "How long?" I asked sadly. "Not long at all" she replied, "but don't worry Knight, my friends Bravoo and Fendi will look after you".

Then Daengseed looked into my eyes and became very serious.

"A man will come looking for me. He has many names; some call him Guy, some call him Mr Two-Legs or Mr Pyjama and the Behaviourists call him Mr Blue. He will be very sad when he hears that I am gone. You must promise me, my dear friend, to look after this man and to help him to become happy again. Please, please promise me this".

After all that Daengseed had done for me, I was more than happy to do everything possible to fulfill this commitment whatever it took, although I did not fully understand what I could do to help. The following evening Dr Su came and cradled Daengseed in her arms; then she took her away. As they passed, Daengseed smiled peacefully at me; her tail wagging, albeit very weakly. "Remember your promise, my dear, brave, faithful friend" she whispered and then they left.

I never saw Daengseed again; but I still feel her presence within me to this day.

Chapter 17

A lucky break

The weeks that followed were the saddest of my life. Never had I
felt so alone and despite the very best efforts of Bravoo and Fendi,
I was miserable. I had to remind myself, repeatedly, that Bravoo
and Fendi had known Daengseed for so much longer than me and
this thought drew us all closer. Without Bravoo and Fendi and my
regular visits from Curtis, I am not sure how I would have coped.

Life goes on however and a few months later, in November
2019, I was being walked by a lady called Kat, which I thought was
a very strange name for a two-legs. Although she didn't actually
meow, she did purr and she was very kind to me. She had blond
hair and very brightly coloured long nails; so perhaps she really
did think she was a cat? Anyhow, we had some lovely walks
together and occasionally she would sing which I rather liked. At
Soi Dog all we dogs have 'Top Trumps' cards showing our photo,
our gender, our age and describing our status. I was listed as a shy
dog and my card said that walkers would have to be patient with
me and slowly build my confidence. Some were good at this and
some not so good. Although well-meaning, humans have a habit
of cuddling we dogs and this unnerves many of us, especially when
we don't know them. If only humans would look at the photos they
take while cuddling us, they would see that often we are looking

away and that usually we are looking extremely uncomfortable!

Happily Kat (I still cannot get used to this name!) understood this, so our walks were comfortable, fairly stress-free and very trust-building and much to my surprise I was beginning to like her. By "much to my surprise" I mean that, other than Curtis, I had never really liked or trusted a human before ... and now I liked two!

Then one day she disappeared, or rather she didn't appear in the morning. I think it was a Wednesday or a Thursday and for the balance of the week I had no more walks. As you can imagine, I was quite distressed as I really liked Kat and I felt comfortable with her. She was always very kind to me and her walks were my highlight of the day. Furthermore, I was really worried for her as she didn't seem to me to be the type of person to just disappear. I was eventually to discover that she had fallen in the shower and had badly broken her wrist. This had required a spell in hospital and some bed rest as her arm was in a cast.

Kat eventually came back to Soi Dog and when she did I hardly noticed (for which I now feel quite guilty), but Daengseed's words had come true as, somehow, I always knew they would:

"A man will come looking for me. He has many names; some call him Guy, some call him Mr Two-Legs or Mr Pyjama and the Behaviourists call him Mr Blue. He will be very sad when he hears that I am gone. You must promise me, my dear friend, to look after this man and to help him to become happy again. Please promise me this".

Chapter 18
...the Behaviourists call him Mr Blue

Since I had last heard these magical words, I had had many disappointments. The word "guy" came up in conversation all the time at Soi Dog. I remember when I first heard someone say "He's such a nice guy" my body went rigid. Had Guy arrived? How would I recognise him? What if he didn't notice me? What could I do to make him happy? What if I let Daengseed down? But I soon came to understand that a guy wasn't The Guy and every time I would be enveloped in sadness. As much as I loved Soi Dog and as much as I appreciated all that they had done for me, which included saving my life let's not forget, I felt that I had a pre-determined destiny and that this destiny was something to do with a man called Guy. But who was Guy and would I ever meet him? If only I could talk to the humans, I could ask for advice, but with only "woof" on my CV, I just felt so helpless.

To explain what happened on Monday 2nd December, I first have to go back in time to just after my accident, when I was being looked after by Curtis. Apparently humans have what they call 'days off' and when Curtis had a day off I would be looked after by two other behaviourists. One was called Eve (whose real name is Sujidtra) and the other was called Mr O (whose real name is Varudh). They were both very special and Curtis had told me to trust them, so I did. More to the point, and unbeknown to me at the time, Mr O had a private nickname for the man I was looking for.

Returning to November, Kat's place was taken by a younger human called Elle. In the last week of November, during our Friday walk, Elle said to me: "We have a new volunteer walking with us next week, Knight. He's been here before although you were in hospital during his last visit. I am so much looking forward to meeting him as everyone says he's a really nice guy."

It seems strange to me now that this weekend was just like other weekends. The volunteers all take Saturday and Sunday off so that they can play together and, of course, most of the Soi Dog staff also take time out so that they can be with their family and friends. The Sanctuary doesn't close altogether as we have to be fed and watered (and cleaned up after, but I won't elaborate on that), so there is a skeleton staff on hand. Also, as Soi Dog is famous around the world, it is open to visitors on Saturday morning. That said, we dogs tend to lounge about and do nothing much. Yes, we miss our walks but we understand the needs of humans to spend time with other humans and we allow for this without too much of a fuss. All of which brings me on to Monday 2nd December.

The day started like any other. Elle turned up at 09:00, well organised and ready to go and just behind her was a human that I didn't recognise. This must be the new guy, I thought to myself. I do hope he is kind. He seemed a bit flustered to me. He was carrying his kit bag but the dog leads were hanging out. Furthermore, he had a rather cumbersome, old fashioned camera which banged from side to side as he ran to catch up with Elle. He was much older than Elle and he had gingery grey hair, some of which must have fallen out as there were bits missing. His sunglasses were lopsided and held together with sticky tape and an off-cut from a drinking straw (quite clever actually); and he was very white. His whiteness was accentuated by the fact that he was dressed all over in dark blue. Blue shirt, blue shorts, blue socks (thankfully short) and blue shoes. Only his hat was another colour. This was a creamy grey and attached to it was a slightly rusted 'Soi Dog volunteer' badge. To my untrained eye, he seemed a bit of a mess but he had the air of someone very comfortable with himself. He very politely introduced himself to Elle, looking her steadily in the eye: "Hello, I'm Guy", he said and then he did the same with Mo, our carer. When saying hello to Mo he shook him firmly by the hand. I had seen humans do this, but I had never seen a volunteer greet a carer with such warmth before. He then went off to find Khun Doe, our chief carer, and he gave her a huge big hug which was a bit of a shock to me as all us dogs were a bit wary of Doe and tended to keep our distance! Although his teeth were a bit crooked (we dogs notice things like this), he had a nice smile and I felt that I could like him in time. I had noticed that he had called himself Guy, but I didn't take much notice of this as all the guys seemed to be guys, if that makes sense.

Then he did something rather strange. He entered our run (in the process causing mayhem for Mo by letting a few dogs escape into the airlock) and he started looking around. He was clearly familiar with a number of the dogs and he greeted them all by name, giving them a little tickle as he passed them by; he kept looking around, almost as if lost, but clearly not lost. I noticed that he made a very special fuss of both Bravoo and Fendi, but he remained unsettled. It seemed to me that he was looking for someone or something but, before I had the chance to think much more about it, our walk routine started. As one of the shyer dogs, I am quite far down on the walking pecking order. This doesn't mean that my walk is in any way second rate, but the boisterous dogs get to go out first, so I never walk until the afternoon. Strangely, I found myself very unsettled throughout the morning. This new human confused me. Something was clearly unsettling and there was a strange vibe in the air but, try as I might, I couldn't put my paw on it.

At lunch time, all the volunteers go to the fabulous new Volunteer & Visitor Centre for lunch. We dogs are not allowed in this building but we pass it during our walks and it is very smart indeed. And if you are lucky enough to be on the first post-lunch walk, you get to sense all sorts of delicious smells, although this can be a bit frustrating as you never get to taste any of these smells! So you can imagine my surprise when I saw our new human head towards the Administration block rather than the Visitor Centre at lunchtime. When I next saw him he was clearly distressed, his eyes were red and his body drooped. His confident air had disappeared and he looked more like a deflated balloon and, even though I had yet to meet him, I felt desperately sorry for him. There was something about this human that really moved me.

The day progressed and, when it came to my walk time, I was disappointed that the new human chose to walk with Pieno (whom he had met the previous year), rather than myself. I think that Elle had also picked up on his distress as they walked together quite closely and talked quietly and, at one stage, I thought I heard him mention Daengseed and my heart skipped a little beat. "Don't be silly" I said to myself, "This couldn't be the man, surely? He doesn't even look like the man" but then I stopped as, once again, I remembered that I had no idea what the man looked like. That night I took myself off to a quiet corner in our run and settled down to a troubled night's sleep. Thankfully I woke with a clear head and I decided to put Daengseed and the new two-legs out of my mind and to simply concentrate on the day at paw.

That morning I was surprised to see Mr O, the Behaviourist, milling around the entrance to our run as the Behaviourists rarely came to visit us. It's not that they ignore us, but rather they are always so busy helping dogs like me (as I once was) come to terms with humans. Anyhow, there he was, leaning up against the fence, clearly waiting to meet someone. In the distance I could see the new human approaching and I realised with interest that he was walking directly towards Mr O with a big smile on his face.

Obviously they had met before, almost certainly the previous year. Then I heard them talk and suddenly I found that I could hardly breathe. My body started to shake all over and my vision went blurry. It was as though an electric shock had passed right through me, from the tip of my ears down to my paws. My senses were all awry and my body felt that it was shutting down. I was so dizzy and faint that I had to sit before I fell over. I couldn't believe what I had heard but I knew that it was very real. Mr O had just run up to our new human with a big smile and said, quite clearly: "Mr Blue! How wonderful to see you again".

Chapter 19

Tuesday 3rd December

Oh-My-Dog; this is him, Mr Blue, the man they call Guy. This is the man that Daengseed talked of with her final breath. He had come back to find her, just as she said he would. How did she know? How could she have been so sure? Suddenly I felt myself crying; I was just so overwhelmed with what I had seen and heard. Mr Blue had travelled over 6,000 miles to find my friend Daengseed and she was no longer with us. No wonder he looked so distressed yesterday afternoon. What was I to do?

My mind was completely blank, my body had shut down, I was drained and all the other dogs were looking at me strangely. I realised that if I didn't move I might be taken for injured or weak and that's not a good thing in a pack, so I forced myself back up onto my paws. Right at the back of the A3 run there is an area for shy dogs and this is where I headed, as far from the action as possible. Finding myself a quiet corner, I lay down to think. What would Daengseed have done had the roles been reversed? I am quite sure she would have taken up the challenge of attracting Mr Blue's attention somehow ... if only I could think of a way to do this!

For once I was glad that I was a quiet dog and so not expected to walk until the afternoon. Instead I watched from afar as Elle and

Mr Blue started their walk routine. Mr Blue harnessed Juturna (our alpha) and Elle took out Mongju. Next Mr Blue paired with Aylin while Elle walked Baoviwe. And so the pattern continued, except that there was no pattern. Or was there? It seemed to me that when Mr Blue knew one of the dogs from the pair being walked, he favoured that dog. Catching up with old friends, I think you humans call it!

After a while a germ of an idea came to me, and a tingle of excitement ran down my spine! We dogs are always walked in pairs and the pairing is carefully thought out so as to avoid any canine clashes. I usually walked with Pieno as she was another quiet dog, so first I needed to seek her support as I reckoned Mr Blue would continue to walk Pieno rather than me (as they were old friends).

So off I trotted to find Pieno. "Are there any dogs in our run who were here last year and didn't like walking with the new human?" I asked Pieno hopefully. After a moment's thought she replied "Yes there is one. Hadad. For some reason, Hadad was a bit wary of him last year. They walked together once, or at least they tried to but half way around the walk Hadad sat down and refused to budge. So this human of yours picked him up and carried him back to base, which would have been fine with me but Hadad felt a bit trapped in his arms and so avoided him thereafter." Hmmm. I knew that Arlena usually paired with Hadad during walks ... yes, this could work!

All the volunteers think that Arlena is a really sweet dog, but we dogs know that she has a bit of a short temper and is prone to causing trouble and then sneaking off. Her sweet, innocent looks often mean that some other dog gets the blame for an incident started by Arlena and although it was not in my nature to plays tricks on anyone, if I had to trick any dog in A3 it would be Arlena!

Happily for me, Pieno was eager to help and come the moment she timed her move to perfection. Mr Blue and Elle had just returned with Bravoo and Fendi, and Mo (the A3 carer) had ushered Hadad and Arlena towards the airlock-doors in preparation for their walk. Just as he opened the inner door to let them through, Pieno rudely 'bumped' into Arlena who turned around with a growl and, while she was distracted, I snuck into the airlock with Hadad!

"Ah" said Mr Blue to Elle, "Hadad doesn't really like me, I had best take this other dog. What's he called by the way?" Thanks to Pieno, my little plan had worked a treat and I was about to take my first walk with Mr Blue. I thought of my friend Daengseed and all the lovely walks that she had enjoyed with him last year, of the stories she had told me and of the bond that had formed between them ... and of all the hopes that they had shared for the future; and again I remembered her words:

"You must promise me, my dear friend, to look after this man and to help him to become happy again. Please promise me this".

Chapter 20

Would you like to live in England?

The next week or so was a bit of a blur, other than I walked with Mr Blue every day which was quite wonderful. Daengseed had told me that Mr Blue talked to her during walks and this is what I remembered best. I just loved his voice and how he spoke to me as if I was his best friend. First he introduced himself; "How nice to meet you Knight. My name is Guy and I come from England. You can call me Guy. Even though I know you only speak "woof" I reckon you dogs are far smarter than most humans think ... and I have lots of questions to ask you!".

So started the most exciting period of my life to date. I soon discovered that Mr Blue was a big softie, albeit a softie with an embedded anger about the many injustices of this world. He loved talking about his children and, strangely, comparing them to dogs we both knew. His daughter Scarlett reminded him of Forge (or Forgie as he rather bravely called him), one of our more stubborn sanctuary residents! This confused me as Forge is a mighty and very powerful dog, but Mr Blue explained that walking Forge was always a challenge, rather like debating with his daughter. "We don't always agree, in fact we often disagree, but never an angry word between us!" he said, although I am not sure whether he was referring to Forge or Missy Scarlett! Next he told me that his sons

William and Jack reminded him of Bravoo and Preyta as they were inseparable friends. This made far more sense to me as the Bravoo/Preyta bromance was famous in Soi Dog circles. Sadly it came to an end earlier in the year when Preyta was offered adoption. At first he didn't want to leave his friend, but Bravoo persuaded him that it was the opportunity of a lifetime and that he had to take it. In my mind Bravoo has never been the same since, I think it rather broke his heart saying goodbye to Preyta, but Bravoo is the most honourable dog I have ever met ... and he did the right thing by persuading Preyta to leave. Sadly, Bravoo cannot be adopted as he has kidney issues. This is lovingly managed by the Soi Dog medical team, but it does mean that Bravoo will stay at the sanctuary for the rest of his life. Like all of us, he is so grateful to Soi Dog for saving his life and he has long ago accepted his fate, making the most of every day. A quite exceptional CARPE DIEM dog is my friend Bravoo!

I think it must have been on our third or fourth walk together that Mr Blue first asked me about Daengseed. I am ashamed to say that, in my new-found euphoric state, I had rather forgotten about Daengseed and my promise to her; and the very mention of her name brought me firmly down to earth. "Did you ever get to meet my lovely Daengseed?" he asked and never before have I so desperately wanted to be able to speak "human". I so much wanted to shout YES at the top of my bark and tell him about all the fun we had together. I wanted to tell him how Daengseed had protected me when I joined the A3 run, and how she introduced me to Bravoo and Fendi; but most of all I wanted to say: "Yes, I knew Daengseed and she talked about you all the time. She told us that you would return ... and she never lost heart. She loved you so much; she just knew that you would come for her". I also wanted to tell him how dignified she had been at the end; and to say that her last woofs were all about you, Mr Blue, her true love.

Instead all I could do is look at him sadly. He had stopped

walking and he had a tear running down his cheek. He looked back at me and suddenly his face lit up: "You knew her well, didn't you!" he exclaimed; "I just know it. In fact I think you were very special friends, perhaps even the best of friends!". Then he knelt down on the ground and kissed me gently on my head.

That night I had an urgent conversation with Bravoo. "How do you get adopted?" I asked my friend. "You're asking the wrong dog" said Bravoo with a wry grin; "But I do remember Preyta telling me that it just happened. If a human likes you enough and if you are suitable for adoption and if you are healthy and if you are lucky, then you might be adopted". It seemed to me that there were far too many "if"s in this sentence and, once again, I had a troubled night's sleep. I dreamt that I was trapped in the building in Soi Thummasopa and that Mr Blue was calling for me with some urgency. "Come on Knight, come on. We really do have to go" he was saying, but I was stuck fast and I just couldn't get out ...

My joyous new life continued. Although I was an afternoon walker, Mr Blue called in to see me every morning and often stayed to chat with me when the walking was over in the afternoon. That said, he continued to talk with and tickle all the dogs, but it seemed to me that he spent just a few minutes more with me than with the others. His human walking partner was still Elle but now, when we walked with Pieno, Elle took Pieno's lead. I am forever grateful to Pieno for so readily accepting this swap over of human walking partners as it can't have been easy for her as Mr Blue and Pieno were old friends. Of course, because we walked as a foursome, Pieno still had many opportunities to schmooze with my human, especially when we stopped in the shade for a breather and a sit down ... but I was getting the lion's share of his attention.

13 December 2019

It was a particularly hot Friday and even us Asian dogs were slightly on edge. Not only because it was hot but also because it was a Friday and we don't get walked over the weekends as staff and volunteers need time off to relax. Mr Blue popped in to see me just before 09:00 as usual and I noticed that he had an especially wide grin on his face. "Good morning Knight" he beamed, "I have something special to ask you". Whether or not he planned to ask me there and then I don't know as, just at that moment, Juturna got the barkies and Mo chucked a bucket of water over him, most of which landed on my human! Mr Blue laughed it off, muttering "Lucky it's a hot day, eh Mo, I'll be dry in a few minutes!" Then he winked at me and said "Let's talk later, Knighty" before disappearing off for his first walk of the day.

I did wonder what he wanted to ask me, but I didn't think that much of it at the time as he was always asking me questions. What did I think of this, what did I think of that etc? He never tired of questions but he did say it was special, so I found myself getting more and more excited as my walk time approached. Although a shy boy, I somehow found the courage to barge my way to the front of the queue that always forms by the air lock at walk changeover time (approx every 20 minutes). "Steady on Knight, old pup" said Bravoo, then he smiled his beautiful smile; "You really do love that human, don't you!" he teased.

It was still an intensely hot day and so Mr Blue and Elle led us to a shady spot where we could sniff around and lie in the grass if we wanted to. Elle kept looking at Mr Blue and nudging him; there was something in the air and she seemed particularly happy which was nice to see. I remember sitting very close to Mr Blue, which I would never normally do, and looking at him as if so say: "Well???" And then he said it: "Knight, would you like to come and live in England with me?". Of course I had no idea what this meant but Elle was jumping up and down shouting: "Mr Knight's been adopted, Mr Knight's been adopted" and Pieno was running around in circles chasing her tail. Now if there's one word we Soi Dogs do know it is "adopted" and I suddenly realised the enormity of the situation. Mr Blue was offering to take me home with him, to start a new life in England.

I looked up into the sky and I am sure that I saw Daengseed looking down at me, tail wagging furiously. She looked quite magnificent, all her scars had gone, her legs were toned and strong and her coat was shining bright. I closed my eyes to capture the moment and quietly woofed "Thank you Daengseed" to the best friend I had ever had.

It was, quite simply, the happiest moment of my young life.

Chapter 21

Covid hits Thailand

For the next two weeks Mr Blue and I made plans. He told me all about his house in England and he warned me that England would not be so warm. I didn't really know what a house was and I had certainly never been in one, but it sounded wonderful. As to the temperature, not-so-warm sounded good to me too!

One day Mr Blue told me all about Kimba, his previous rescue dog. She had been found with a length of wire tied tightly around her tail, cutting off the blood supply and causing her tail to die. What agony she must have been in, poor pup. When her owner was asked "Why?" he simply replied "When her tail falls off she'll look like one of those pedigree dogs and then I'll sell her". Happily for Kimba (or Josephine as she was at the time) she was taken to a shelter where she met Mr Blue's children and, soon after, was adopted by Mr Blue's family. I looked up at "my human" as I was beginning to think of him, as if to ask why he had re-named Josephine. "You're probably wondering why I changed her name" he mused. "Well I was born in Northern Nigeria where they speak a language called Hausa. When we collected Josephine she was tiny and she sat on my lap all the way home gazing into my eyes. Quite simply, she was the most beautiful small animal I had ever seen and so I called her Karama Kimba, which means beautiful small animal in Hausa." I wonder if he'll change MY name I thought to myself? "As you're coming to England with me I thought I might call you Mr Knight, old thing. What do you think? It sounds rather good to me!". And from that moment on, everyone started to call me Mr Knight!

On Friday 27 December my human took me for two walks, the first with Elle and Baoviwe (as Pieno wasn't feeling well) and the second, much to my surprise, just by myself. He seemed a bit low which worried me and soon I discovered why: "I have to go home tomorrow" he said sadly, "and we're not going to see each other for three months while we wait for your adoption and medical tests to be processed." As always, I had no idea what this meant but I knew it wasn't good news, and I prayed to Daengseed that he wasn't cancelling my adoption. Somehow I knew this wasn't the case, but I couldn't think why else our happy time had so suddenly turned so sombre.

At some stage Khun Doe came out looking for us as we had exceeded our allocated walk time and the shelter was preparing for evening shut-down. As we walked back to A3 my human perked up and appeared quite jolly, but by now I had got to know him well and I could tell it was a bit of an act. Again he knelt and kissed me gently on my head ... "Be patient, we'll see each other again soon" he said, and then he disappeared from my life.

The next few weeks were miserable and I rather lost my confidence. Certainly I kept myself to myself and Khun Mo had to come and find me in the run and almost drag me out for walks. I really didn't understand what was going on as everyone who came to see me seemed so excited! "You're a lucky dog, Mr Knight" they all said, "You've been adopted and soon you'll be off to England to live with Guy". All I could think of was: Where has my human gone? Why has he left me behind? Did I do something wrong? I looked up into the sky but I couldn't find Daengseed. I was so sad for myself and also worried that I had let Daengseed down.

Happily Elle was still at the shelter, so there was some continuity in my life. When we walked she regularly spoke of Guy, telling me what fun I was going to have in England and how lucky I was. Others came to see me too. In particular Caro, Kat, Annerieke, Katie, Celia, Tini and Tom all seemed to know, or know of, my human and everyone around was so excited for me ... and this kept me going and gave me the confidence to believe that, just maybe, I would see my human again. One day St John himself came to see me. "Hello Mr Knight" he beamed. "Guy has sponsored me to take you out for a nice walk." What came over me I don't know, but I ran away and hid and refused to come out. I think I was just too overwhelmed to cope with this kindest of men coming to visit me. Everyone was smiling, everyone was congratulating me, everyone was talking of Guy; but my human had gone and I was missing him dreadfully.

Days turned into weeks and weeks turned into months. Elle returned home to Sweden and, it seemed to me, that my final link to Mr Blue had broken. Whenever I felt myself giving up hope which, if I'm honest was almost every day, I reminded myself of Daengseed and how she just knew that Mr Blue would return. I was ashamed that I was giving up on a dream that Daengseed absolutely refused to give up on, but I couldn't help it. Some nights I dreamt of Daengseed and our happy times together. On these occasions I usually awoke with her words in my mind: "A man will come looking for me" and this gave me added resolve.

Meanwhile something was very wrong at the sanctuary and it was upsetting all we dogs. Although Soi Dog employs over 250 full time staff, our walking is undertaken by volunteers, all of whom love dogs enough to give up their holidays to walk us. I had now been at the sanctuary for 16 months (including my time in the hospital) and it had always been a hive of activity, but suddenly all the volunteers had gone and we were not being walked, or rather we were only getting one or two short walks a week, rather than a good long walk every day.

Everyone was talking of "Covid" and, at first, we were fearful that this might be a new canine disease that none of us had heard of. But soon it became apparent that Covid was a human disease and that it was killing people. I learned that this awful disease was thought to have originated in a wet market in China, as had so many previous killer diseases. We dogs are terrified of China and with good reason, as the nation kills an estimated 20 million dogs and cats a year for human consumption.

My imagination ran riot inside my head. What if my human catches Covid, I worried. How will I know if he is terribly ill and needs me? The thought that I might arrive in England, only to discover that my human had succumbed to Covid, horrified me. Fortunately this fear of the unknown filled me with resolve and made me somehow stronger. I had to do a Daengseed and never give up.

However, it seemed to me that the clock had stopped. Every minute felt like a day and every day dragged on for a lifetime. Without volunteers there was no one to accompany us adopted dogs to our forever homes and it dawned on me that, perhaps, I was destined to live out my life in the shelter after all. *

With the volunteers gone, Yanisa took on my walking duties. Yanisa was one of the volunteer co-ordinators, so she understood dogs well and knew of my limitations. She also knew my human and mentioned him every time we went for a walk, encouraging me to remain positive which I did my very best to do.

With fewer walks to entertain us, some of the more boisterous dogs were getting restless and a bit frustrated. One day I got caught

---

* Most adopted Soi Dogs travel to their forever destination as "excess baggage" with flight volunteers. These dogs are placed in travel crates in a special "livestock hold" in an airplane. Although the journey is long, and no doubt unnerving, it is safe and the dogs are fed and watered at all stop-offs en route to their forever homes. With Covid-19 and the global travel restrictions that ensued, volunteers could no longer travel in and out of Thailand, meaning that adopted dogs could not accompany them on their return journeys.

up in a fight, or rather I was collateral damage as I think you humans call it. Up to now I had been rather proud of the fact that the only two parts of my body without scars were my head and my bottom; everything in between was marked all over! But now I had a scar on my head courtesy of a bite, but at least my bottom was perfect! Then, blow me down, Khun Doe noticed a small lump on my right hand perineal area, also known as my bum! On 31 March I was admitted to hospital for surgery as the lump had grown to 4cm x 3cm. Post-op histopathology results showed the lipoma to be a (benign) subcutaneous mass which was a relief, but now I had a scar on my bottom too ... what would my human think?

In July I was again admitted to hospital, this time for dental scaling which I thought very odd. I had scars on all four legs and paws, all over my torso, on my head and on my bottom. I had counted 17 scars at least; so why did I need shiny white teeth? Maybe they were just trying to cheer me up and take my mind off what might have been, I thought to myself sadly, as I settled down in my preferred quiet corner of the A3 run that evening.

Then a miracle happened ...

Curtis came to visit me! I was so happy as I hadn't seen him for so long and I was even happier to see that he had a lead in his hand. I bounded up to him and he gave me the biggest grin I have ever seen. "Come with me, Knight" he beckoned, "we have some work to do". But rather than go for a walk, he led me to his office where I saw a big crate. How strange I thought, why is he bringing me here? Then lovely Eve appeared, giggling and full of fun ... and my heart began to beat just a little faster. Something BIG was happening that was causing great joy and, for some reason, I seemed to be the focus of attention. "We've found a way of getting you to England" explained Curtis, "and you'll be travelling within the next two weeks with four other dogs. You're a very lucky boy, you're on your way to your forever home at last!" Although I don't speak human, I just knew what this meant ... and I am quite sure that, for just one millisecond, I saw Daengseed out of the corner of my eye, wagging her tail and grinning at me.

Soon the purpose of the crate became apparent, this was to be MY travel crate, it even had my name on it. Suddenly I got the shakes. Could I cope with the confinement? Would this be entrapment all over again? I knew that England must be a long way away as Mr Blue had not come back to visit me. How long was I going to have to live in this crate? Gently Eve coaxed me in. If I'm honest I am not sure that I would have gone in had it not been for the smell of fresh chicken from within but once inside, and with the chicken eaten, I decided I wanted out! Happily getting out was just as easy as getting in and there was no pain involved, no stake impaled into my chest, no rough edges to shred my body. Eve threw in a couple more treats and I dived in to find them. This time she slowly shut the door while talking softly to me. "You do want to see Mr Blue again, don't you Knight?" she asked. "If so you will have to travel in this crate for a day and a night and another day, but then you will be free forever!" I didn't understand her words but I did understand the importance of what she was saying, so I lay down inside the crate and, much to my surprise, I stopped shaking and started to relax. Although not spacious, the crate was large enough to stand up in and turn around in, so I didn't feel too confined. To my relief, it had windows and a latticed door, which meant that I could see all around me and this helped to calm me down.

The next couple of weeks passed in a flash. I spent most of my time with Bravoo and Fendi and also Pieno, who had joined our little group. Sadly neither Bravoo nor Fendi were on the adoptions list due to health issues, but Pieno was fit and hoping, one day, to be adopted herself.

Friday 31 July 2019
Today I had five very special visitors. Firstly Curtis, Eve and Mr O came to take me for a walk. "Monday's the day, old friend" said

Curtis in a slightly shaky voice. He seemed so happy and yet so sad at the same time. I noticed that Eve was holding his hand and she seemed equally sad. Fortunately Mr O was his usual chirpy self: "Say hello to Mr Blue from me" he said smiling. Next I was visited by St John. Without this man and without his wonderful wife Gill I would not be alive, indeed I would have died a slow and horribly painful death. As before, I was completely overwhelmed in his presence and didn't know quite what to do, so I kept my distance and just wagged my tail furiously, while trying hard to convey the biggest THANK YOU in the world! Finally Khun Doe came to have a word. "You've had a difficult life, Knight" she said to me in Burmese, "and now you have the chance to start again. I know you are a nervous dog and you will come across many scary things in your new life but remember, no one will ever hurt you again and Mr Blue will keep you safe." Then she cried a little bit and gave me a kiss.

That night I snuggled up with Bravoo, Fendi and Pieno. My life at Soi Dog was almost over and I was enveloped with sadness for I was about to say Goodbye to so many very special friends. But a new chapter in my life was about to begin ... and I had fulfilled my promise to my dearest of all friends, the beautiful Daengseed.

Chapter 22

8,000 miles in four days

Monday 03 August 2019

Today started very early indeed and it was still dark when I was awoken. In seconds A3 came alive, you could feel the tension in the air, but the dogs quickly settled after I had been led out. I would have liked some private time with Bravoo, Fendi and Pieno before leaving but this wasn't possible ... it was clear we were on a tight schedule.

Khun Doe took me for a little walk and gave me some breakfast (and a good talking to about being well behaved and upholding Soi Dog's honour etc), before leading me over to a shed that I had not been in before. In this shed were five travel crates; two small, two medium (one of which I recognised as mine) and one really big crate. My heart was beating like you wouldn't believe as Doe encouraged me into my crate and locked the door behind me.

Had I been a human, I might well have drawn an analogy between my situation and that of Yuri Gagarin being strapped into his tiny Vostok capsule, before being catapulted at huge velocity into space and a journey of the almost unknown. The only difference being that Mr Gagarin was fully briefed, knew what he was doing and had trained for the occasion!

The fact is, I am not a human and I do not have particularly advanced cognitive skills. Rather I am a soi (street) dog from Phuket in Thailand and so, at this stage in my extraordinary story, I feel it's right to pause for a reality check.

I have just been enclosed in a travel crate and I have absolutely no idea why, although the people who put me in it have always been very kind to me, so I don't feel in any great danger. I didn't really know that I had been adopted and that I was about to fly to England to spend the rest of my life with Mr Blue. I am just a dog remember!

Yes, I was trapped for four days and five nights in a derelict building and my body was shredded as I tried in vain to escape. I remember that only too well, it is fact. As is my time in the Soi Dog hospital with the wonderful team that saved my life. Although I never actually read my medical records (I didn't need to, I could feel the pain), the details of my injuries are taken from the hospital records, so the details of my recovery are accurate. I most definitely know and love Curtis, I am very fond of Eve and Mr O and I know Khun Doe and Khun Mo from A3. I have met John Dalley, although I wouldn't have known who he was; and on both occasions I had been overwhelmed in his presence. Of course I knew Daengseed, Bravoo, Fendi, Pieno and all the A3 pack. I even remember a volunteer who talked to me every day for the best part of a month (he had a very distinctive voice), before he disappeared as all volunteers do. But I don't honestly know that I have been adopted ... and I have absolutely no idea why I've been put in a crate!

What I do know is that I am with four other dogs; Holden, Alleye, Simba (also known as Bornham and soon to become Elvis!) and Princess Daphne (yes, you've guessed it, the Princess is in the large travel crate although, to be fair, she is larger than the rest of us!).

Although I am trying to be brave, I am scared witless as are my fellow travellers. We are all whimpering a bit, but having four other dogs in the same predicament is somehow comforting. This and the fact that all the humans around us are super cheerful and excited. Whatever is happening, I think it must be a good thing, however confusing it is.

Next, we are all loaded onto the back of a truck, a bit like the one that brought me to Soi Dog those many moons ago and then, with a jolt, we are off. I hear rather than see people cheering, and I recognise Curtis' voice above all the others: "Have a safe journey brave Knight, and be happy." Then our truck accelerates and the voices, the cheering and the clapping fade into the distance. Whatever was happening, wherever we were going, we were on our way.

Soi Dog shelter to Phuket International Airport (HKT)

...and ten minutes later we had arrived. How strange, I thought, we could have walked to this place rather than travelled in crates on the back of a van. Little did I know what was to come!

An airport is a scary place for a shy dog like me, actually all five of us were on edge, even Princess Daphne. Outside, cars were racing about and tooting, people were shouting and vans (such as ours) were making strange beeping noises as they reversed into small gaps next to signs that read: UNLOADING ONLY - MAXIMUM STAY 5 MINUTES.

"I need a pee" I thought to myself, "when are we going to be let out of our crates?" but, rather than being given our freedom, we were loaded onto trolleys and taken through a door that said LIVESTOCK CARGO. Here the kind people wearing Soi Dog shirts said goodbye to us and wished us all a safe journey. I had heard Curtis say the same and I wished someone would explain to me what a "safe journey" actually meant. Then the Soi Dog people waved and left; and we were on our own. Although I was, once upon a time, a feral street dog, I had got used to Soi Dog life and this was the first time in 21 months that I hadn't been under the Soi Dog umbrella. I think it fair to say that we were all quite scared, scared of the unknown that is, but we Soi Dogs are fairly stoic and so we kept ourselves to ourselves, albeit we were very much on edge.

Nok Air flight No. DD7503.
Phuket to Don Mueang Airport, Bangkok
Next we were loaded onto a very strange looking vehicle, the likes of which I had never seen before. It had lots of very small wheels and two huge wings; not feathered bird wings but metal wings. We were put in a very small, softly lit room and I remember that it was quite cool which was nice, as previously we had been a bit hot. I looked around and didn't see any other animals, just me and my new pack of friends. Our crates were well strapped down and I was just about to ask everyone if they had any idea what was happening when, without warning, there was a loud, mechanical whine which turned to a deafening scream and I felt myself being pulled off my feet. The room we were in shook so badly that I began to think that we might die and, just as I was about to howl at the top of my bark, the shaking stopped and I suddenly felt myself get a lot heavier. I think, to be honest, we were all in a state of shock and we were probably all howling or whimpering, but soon the noise morphed from terrifying scream to a deep throated but still noisy drone and we all began to relax just a little bit. And strangely, I stopped feeling heavy ...

"My goodness me" said Princess Daphne, "whatever was that? I really did think that my heart might burst right through my chest!" Simba, who had been very quiet up to this moment suggested that it might have been a hurricane, while Holden and Alleye were convinced that we were caught up in a tsunami. Whatever was going on, none of us seemed hurt in any way and although it probably sounds rather daft, I had a strange sense of floating through the sky like a bird!

Being in travel crates, there was nothing we could do, so we settled down to wait and see what would happen next. My heart was certainly thumping and I still needed a pee, but there was no way I was going to soil my little crate, so I just hung on! Then, out of the blue, after quite some time, the tone of background noise changed and suddenly there was a big thump, following by more mechanical screaming, before we came to a stop. The next thing I remember is being unloaded from the big, strange vehicle before being loaded onto a van ... with an orange Soi Dog logo on it. By now I was very confused; had something gone awry? Were we being taken back to the shelter?

Whatever was going on, the people who had collected us were very kind and we were all fed chicken through our lattice doors before we set off on the next stage of our journey. After 30 minutes or so in the van we arrived at Chatuchak, just north of Bangkok at what I soon discovered was a satellite Soi Dog clinic, albeit tiny compared to the huge Phuket shelter I had been living in.

Here, at last, we were allowed out of our crates to pee and poo and then we all went for a welcome walk together before settling down for the afternoon. It had been a long day and we were tired and confused and happy to snooze and finally, to fall sleep as the sun set on our total and complete muddlement.

Nothing much happened the next day, which added to our confusion as, by now, the five of us felt that we were on a mission of sorts! We were beginning to get to know each other and we were all asking: Why were we here? Was this the end of our journey? And, if so, what purpose had it served? I rather assumed that we were now in England which really confused me as it didn't seem that different to Thailand! Just as we were coming to accept this new life, on a Wednesday afternoon if I recall, the five of us were rounded up, returned to our travel crates, loaded back on the Soi Dog van and driven to Suvarnabhumi International Airport.

Wednesday 5th August 2019
Qatar Airways flight No. QR835.
Bangkok to Hamad International Airport, Doha
There seemed to be a pattern developing here as, once again, we were unloaded from the van and put on trollies. Again we were wheeled

through a big door that said LIVESTOCK CARGO and again our Soi Dog friends bade us farewell and wished us a safe onward journey. However we were now in an altogether much bigger room and I could smell and hear other animals whining.

After what seemed like a very long time we were loaded onto another strange looking vehicle with metal wings, this even bigger than the last. I could smell horse and I definitely heard a cat meow, so we were not alone, not that this was any consolation. In time we again heard a mechanical whine which developed into a fearful roar. As before, after a very bumpy minute or so, I suddenly felt that strange floating/flying sensation return to me. It was all very unsettling, and I could hear Princess Daphne tut-tutting as if to say "Not again!". Our crates all had two bowls each fixed inside the doors and, before loading, these had been filled with food and water. Being in a state of some anxiety, my throat was rather dry, so I edged forwards and had a drink.

Fortunately we dogs have a fairly relaxed attitude towards time, as long as we are not left alone for too long. Which is just as well as this leg of our journey seemed to me to go on forever. Initially I was constantly trying to adjust my position to accommodate my back legs but, eventually, I settled down to snooze. Princess Daphne seemed very relaxed and comfortable to me but Holden, Alleye and Simba were quite restless, much like myself. We tried to chat a among ourselves but the loud drone, which seemed to emanate from outside our room, made communication almost impossible, which was a shame as there was nothing else to do. After what seemed like an eternity to me, the noise outside changed and we felt a big bump, before grinding to a halt. Although I had no idea what was happening, where we were or why, I did notice one thing; when the door to our room was opened we were assaulted by a tremendous heat. Not the sort of sticky heat that I was used to at Soi Dog, but an altogether dryer and more oppressive heat. I didn't like it and was pleased when we were trollied off (yet again!) into yet another (cooler) holding area.

"Really, this is becoming just a little bit tiresome" said Princess Daphne and the rest of us couldn't help but agree. We were all a bit tetchy and we needed a walk and a pee, but, to our dismay, there was no sign of us being released from our crates. On the plus side Doha has a wonderful animal care team who came over and checked that we were okay before topping up our water and food supplies. To make matters worse, the horses were being trotted about and brushed down and we had to watch all of this from behind bars in our crates!

It was about now that I remembered Eve's words: "You will have to travel in this crate for a day and a night and another day, but then you will be free forever!" and I passed on this comment to the pack.

"Noooo way!" said Alleye. "You're pulling my tail, surely?" said Holden. "Bollox to that!" said Simba. "Settle down boys" said Princess Daphne, "there's not much we can do about it, so let's not get too worked up". And, of course, she was right ... so we all settled down, happy that the Doha team had put our crates in a circle so that we could all see and comfort each other.

Thursday 6th August 2019
Qatar Airways flight No. QR885.
Doha to Heathrow, London

Back at Soi Dog, it seemed so long ago now, I had heard two volunteers talking about a film called Groundhog Day. In this adventure a man had become trapped in a time loop, meaning that he had relived the same day repeatedly. I was beginning to think this was happening to us as, once again, we were trollied to another large vehicle with metal wings. At first everything about Thursday 6th August seemed the same as Wednesday 5th August, that is until, after hours of constant droning, we felt another big bump and we eventually stopped moving. This time when the doors opened, it was cool, verging on cold and the air smelt very sweet.

Once again we were trollied off (Princess Daphne was not impressed) and this time we were taken to a place called the ARC

(Heathrow Animal Reception Centre) which was full of animals and all sorts of smells that I did not recognise. Smells aside, it seemed that we were causing quite some disturbance: "We can't fit the large crate in our van" I heard a man wail into his telephone, to which a lady replied; "You were given Princess Daphne's crate dimensions a week ago, so maybe you need to find another, altogether bigger van!"

To be honest I had a far greater issue to deal with as I was still desperate for a pee! Throughout the journey, which seemed to have gone on for a lifetime, our water and food bowls had been regularly topped up and I now really needed to relieve myself of all that I had imbibed! To my dismay I heard the man reply: "Okay lady, we'll get another van but you'll have to wait a few hours". On no, I thought and I heard a similar groan from the other four crates.

In time we were loaded onto two trucks. Holden, Alleye and Simba on one and Princess Daphne and myself on the other. It was getting dark now and we had indeed been travelling for a day, a night and another day ... with another night fast approaching.

After what seemed like an eternity the vans parked up and, just as I was about to make some sarcastic comment to Princess Daphne along the lines of "What now?!?" I heard a voice; a voice that I was beginning to think I would never hear again:

"Welcome to England Mr Knight!" said Mr Blue and I honestly thought that my heart would explode with joy.

Chapter 23

Reunited with my human

To say that I was overwhelmed would be an understatement. I was overwhelmed, overcome, overjoyed, over the moon, over absolutely everything. I was looking directly into the eyes of Mr Blue, my very own human, as he smiled back at me and squeezed a sliver of chicken through my latticed front door! "How very, very nice to see you again, old boy" he said "It's been far too long, hasn't it?" and I so much wanted to bark back "Absolutely, old chap, but well worth the wait."

Meanwhile, my tail was swinging from side to side so vigorously that I feared it might fall off, but at that moment I really didn't care because I was in England with Mr Blue. I had never been so happy and strangely, I almost felt as if I had come home, such was my sense of belonging.

While I was becoming reacquainted with Mr Blue, our crates were being unloaded from the vans and taken into my human's house. I noticed that it was dark outside and very quiet, so it must have been deep into the night. By quiet I mean that I could hear no animals, but there was a lot of chatter which suggested that there were lots of humans in the vicinity of our crates. I had never been in a house before and I should have been taking in my surroundings but, to be honest, I had just remembered that I was bursting for a pee and a poo and I really wanted to get out of my crate and relieve myself.

However it very soon became apparent that, although we were in my human's house, someone else was in charge and everyone was deferring to her. As far as I could tell, we were going to be de-crated one at a time, starting with Alleye. This was because Alleye still had a long journey ahead of her, albeit with her humans in their car. "Oh no" I thought to myself, "Does this mean that I'll be last out as I am already at home?". There was nothing to do but cross my legs, settle down and focus on my human's voice.

"Okay Sarah, what do you want me to do?" I heard him ask. It became immediately apparent that Sarah was the new Khun Doe; knowledgeable and authoritative, but with a kindly manner and a gentle touch. First Alleye, then Holden, then Simba were unloaded, fitted with harnesses and sent on their way with their new humans. I can honestly say, I have never been in a room filled with so much love, as these humans took charge of we Soi Dogs. Like my human, they had all waited months for this moment and, although I was desperate (have I mentioned that?!) I was deeply touched to be a part of this highly charged and emotional experience.

The last to go was Princess Daphne whose new home was just one hour away. "Good luck Mr Knight" she said, "I have a strong feeling that you have fallen on your paws big time!". Then she winked at me and left the house, leaving just me, Mr Blue and Sarah.

"Well done Mr Knight, it's your turn now" said Sarah with a big smile on her face before instructing my human to unlock the door of my crate. "Freedom at last" I thought to myself as I gingerly inched out and looked around for somewhere to pee. Sarah giggled happily and said: "Oh, he says, I've got space to run ..." but all I was thinking was "Where can I pee, where can I pee, where can I pee?" The very last thing I wanted to do was make a mess in my human's house but there seemed no way out and I was in a state.

"Crikey, there is nowhere to pee" I fretted running from room to room while Sarah, who clearly knew us dogs well said; "Oops, I think he's going to ..." which is exactly what I did, even before she had the chance to finish her sentence; the two Ps neatly deposited in my human's hallway!

How embarrassing, but happily neither Sarah nor my human seemed even remotely concerned. Although I had never been in a house before, I somehow knew that what I had done was not best etiquette and I vowed to never again pee or poo in my human's home. Happily I am pleased to say that it hasn't happened since! Meanwhile, I had a house to explore and human to get to know ... wow, how quickly my life was changing!

Although it was the middle of the night, Sarah suggested that we go for a short walk so that I could stretch my legs, take in my new surroundings and attend to any further calls of nature. This involved me being fitted with a bright red harness and an even brighter yellow collar onto which was printed the word NERVOUS. Maybe this is my new name, I thought, as we exited the house. More importantly, I was about to go on my first ever walk as a "pet" dog ... what an adventure I was having.

It was about now, just as we stepped outside, that I suddenly realised how tired I was, far more tired than I had ever been in my life before. I had been on the go for over 40 hours and while I had (and I find this quite hard to admit!) cat-napped during the various flights from Thailand to England, the tension and pressure had been utterly exhausting and now everything was catching up with me. Fortunately Sarah and my human understood this and, after a "quick lap of the block" as Mr Blue called it, we were back inside and discussing sleeping plans.

Chapter 24

Finding my paws in England

As I was soon to discover, my new home had two dog beds, a human sofa, a few comfy chairs and four human beds to sleep in (okay, maybe I'm pushing my luck with the human beds) but I chose the wooden floor for my first night's sleep. Partially because it was what I was used to (as in concrete, wood, tarmac etc) and partially because it was cool and indoors seemed so hot, with no fresh air to cool me. So I slept on the floor, Sarah slept upstairs and my human slept on the sofa downstairs, close to me; as he would continue to do for the first few weeks. In Thailand my nights had been filled with noises; cars and trucks racing by, honking horns, people shouting, dogs barking constantly and so on, but here in England, in my new home, it was eerily silent ... and not surprisingly I fell into a deep, deep sleep.

I don't think I dreamed that night or, if I did, I have no memory of it. What I do remember is being absolutely and totally at peace ... as if I had 'arrived' at the place where I was always meant to be. That said I did wake once in the middle of the night and I panicked a bit as I didn't understand where I was and, as I had never slept "indoors" before, I was a bit disorientated. I remember getting up and tentatively looking around, feeling on edge but not really scared. Then I smelt my human, he was asleep on the sofa and that sense of peace returned and I went back to my little corner and slept ... and slept ... and slept!

My first few days in England are a bit of a blur in my memory, as I was truly exhausted, somewhat stressed and rather tense after my long journey; so I spent most of the time sleeping. I remember waking on Friday morning and seeing Mr Blue, my human, sitting quite close to where I was sleeping. Although he wasn't looking directly at me, I had a feeling that he could see me out of the corner of his eye which was just fine. We dogs are a bit uncomfortable with close eye-to-eye contact and I was happy to watch him out of the corner of my eye too, while still pretending to be asleep. This is quite easy for we dogs as we don't have a large area of 'white' in our eyes, so it is not so simple to see where and at what we are looking. "Hello Mr Knight" he said (I was rumbled, he knew I was awake!), "what would you like for breakfast?". Then I heard a happy laugh "Hello Knighty" said Sarah,"Your first day in England! What adventures await you my friend!". Of course, I didn't know what any of this meant but I could sense the vibe, and the vibe was very happy indeed.

Breakfast turned out to be chicken and rice for me and vegan scrambled eggs and bacon on toast for Mr Blue and Sarah. My human seemed quite apologetic about this although Sarah didn't mind one little bit as she was a vegan too, so didn't eat animal based products. This was something new to me. I had heard the terms "vegetarian" and "vegan" used many times at Soi Dog but I hadn't realised that it referred to humans who didn't eat meat or fish. Secretly I rather hoped that I wouldn't have to become a vegetarian or a vegan but, I was intrigued to discover that some humans voluntarily chose not to eat meat. Hmmm, what would life be like without chicken, I pondered, as I munched my way through breakfast.

I had been wondering about Sarah and whether she was to become my new "plus one" human ... it is fair to say that I was a bit confused as Mr Blue, my human, had never mentioned her to me in Thailand; and it seemed to me that he had told me his life story during our Soi Dog walks. Just as I was pondering this and thinking - Do I really want to share my human? - Sarah said, "It's time for me to go as I have a long journey ahead of me". It turned out that Sarah was the Adoptions Support Manager for Soi Dog UK, which explained why she was so efficient while de-crating all we dogs as we arrived in England. I liked Sarah (very much) and I was sorry to see her go; but I did let out a little sigh of relief as, for now, one human felt about right for me. I now know that many Soi Dogs come to England and go and live with a family immediately, and they love every minute of it, but I was (and still am) a physically damaged and mentally scarred dog that needed to take things very slowly. Happily Mr Blue understood this and, it seemed to me, was in absolutely no rush to introduce me to any other humans at all!

It struck me that England was the perfect temperature. It was delightfully warm and there was a gentle breeze in the air. This breeze carried a myriad of magnificent new smells that I could hardly wait to explore, but exploring was going to have to wait as I was so tired I could hardly stand. What I really wanted to do was to find a soft patch of earth under a shady tree somewhere to de-stress and sleep. "You look to me as though you could sleep for a week", said my human "and I know just the place for you Knighty Knight, so follow me!" With that he led me across a lawn to a far corner of the land surrounding his house and found me a soft spot under a tree, far away from the humans who lived around him. I wanted to say thank you but I must have nodded off as, when I awoke, the sun was high in the sky and my human had re-positioned himself so that I was sleeping in his shadow. "Ah, you're awake at last Knighty" said Mr Blue, "I don't know about you but I'm rather hungry, so let's nip home for a bite to eat" and I realised that I was absolutely ravenous.

This is when we both had the first of many reality checks ...

I have already alluded to the fact that it was a lovely sunny day and this had brought out all the humans, who were sitting around tables chatting to each other. Some were pointing and saying "Look, that must be Mr Knight" and others were shouting, "Come over and join us, Guy". Whatever all this meant I have no idea but it filled me with utter dread and caused me to shake with fear. When I was scared at Soi Dog my friend Curtis used to pick me up and hold me firmly and this always calmed me; and I looked at my human pleading him to do the same ... and that is exactly what he did (I later discovered that Curtis had sent Mr Blue a video showing how to best pick me up, mindful of my injuries). So my human picked me up and held me against his chest. I could feel his heart beating, but not racing, and this calmed me down immediately and he carried me back to his house, going the long way around to avoid the humans. As you can imagine, this whole experience really shook me. For the past 3-4 days I had been living on the edge, stressed beyond imagination, travelling thousands of miles from Thailand to England in huge metal birds and, for some reason, I had rather imagined that meeting Mr Blue again had meant that life would, from now on, be easy. But life is not easy for we street dogs (I still thought of myself as a street dog) and it dawned on me that the conversion from feral dog to pet dog was going to be a real challenge!

The next couple of days followed the pattern of the first, other than my human was getting better organised. We would start with a pre-dawn morning walk (with me in full harness), followed by breakfast (chicken and rice for me, cereal and banana for my human) and then we'd go and sit at the bottom of the garden. Mr Blue now packed a water bowl (for me), a large umbrella for shade, a folding chair (for him) and a good book to read. We were becoming altogether more adept at avoiding humans as my human had circulated a note asking everyone to completely ignore us and to not approach us under any circumstances. When 'the coast was clear' as Mr Blue called it, we would nip home for meals and rest breaks (for him, not me)! Despite all these precautions, I still couldn't find the nerve to actually walk home so, whenever we returned to base, my human picked me up and carried me.

I was beginning to think that I could get used to this life!

One day, after about a week, we were sitting by a table relaxing. human was drinking a G&T (something that he rather enjoys) and I was snoozing when, suddenly, there was a huge CRASH noise. I bolted and my human, being caught unawares, let my leads slip through his hands. In a shot I was gone, across the lawn around the back of his house and up against the fence, desperately looking for a means of escape. My human followed, not running but maybe walking very quickly. He didn't panic and he didn't shout "Knight, stop, stop, stop" as some people might have done. When he saw me gnawing at the fence (I wanted to run and run and run as far from that noise as possible), he sat down and started talking to me in a very calm voice. Without really looking at me, he edged closer and closer and eventually got a hold of one of my leads. Instead of pulling on it, he remained quite still and continued talking to me, knowing that I could no longer escape. Eventually I stopped gnawing at the fence and began to calm down, just a little bit. What was I to do? I had soiled myself badly and was a real mess. I was shaking, I was scared and I needed to feel secure. Much to my surprise, my human picked me up and held me close, while whispering in my ear "It's okay Knighty, it's okay. You are safe with me, I'll never let anyone hurt you". Even I thought that was very brave as I really smelt horrible but, while my shaking subsided, my fear of humans intensified.

As it turned out, a kindly neighbour has seen us relaxing together and had come out with a big sack of kibble. This he then dropped on the table adjacent to us with the intention of saying "This is what we feed our dog with, would you like to try some?"

but the CRASH of the sack hitting the table had put the fear of Doe in me and I was gone.

Needless to say, human and I needed a pretty thorough washing down after the event and, even when I had been cleaned up, I was still too scared to accept a treat.

This is when I first discovered "the study". This was a room in my human's house that was cool, very quiet and somewhat hidden away. As of this moment, this room became my bolt-hole and, for the next few weeks, I spent most of my time hidden away in the study. I loved my new human and I was learning to trust him, but life in a house, surrounded by other houses filled with strange humans, was very different to life in the sanctuary back in Phuket. There I had been surrounded by other dogs and humans in orange t-shirts emblazoned with the words Soi Dog, all of whom really understood we dogs.

My new den (aka the study) was located at one end of a small hallway, at the foot of the stairwell. This meant that visitors entering the house (thankfully not that many) could go straight through to the living room without going anywhere near me in the study. When the coast was clear (I was learning the lingo) I would sometimes sneak out but, in the main, my human came into the study and sat on the floor near to me and either talked to me or, if I was snoozing, he read a book.

One day, maybe two weeks into my new adventure, Mr Blue said; "We have to go to work tomorrow, Knighty. This means that you've got to be very brave and travel with me in my van; and then get to know a new space. Don't worry", he added "you and I will be the only people in the building for now; although in time it might fill up again".

Up until this moment, I hadn't thought much about what my human did before I arrived and the concept of "going to work" every day did not particularly appeal to me. Not that I knew what work was, but I had been settling into a routine that had helped me feel secure and I didn't relish the thought of giving that up so quickly.

Seeing my concern, Mr Blue said: "Don't worry Knighty because right now we are going on an altogether different adventure ... your first proper walk!"

For this to make sense, you have to understand where we (me and Mr Blue) lived. Our home was the converted wing of a former school for children with disabilities; specifically, the house we lived in was once the boys' dormitory. Mr Blue likes to tell his friends that he lives in Ian Dury's old home, which indeed he does as Mr Dury (a polio victim) lived here when he was a young boy. Being a school, the grounds are quite spacious (five acres in total), so during my first two weeks we stayed "on-site" which, to me, was just fine. But now Mr Blue was suggesting that we ventured further afield and I wasn't so sure!

The photo on the front of this book was taken on my very first outside walk! I remember being both hugely excited and even more nervous as we opened the gate and "stepped outside". In hindsight I needn't have worried as there were far fewer people per acre outside than in, but we were stepping out beyond my comfort zone and that gave me the shakes. I remember stopping every ten metres or so to look behind me and to check that Mr Blue was still with me, which was silly really as we were both at opposite ends of my leads, so never that far apart! Of course, quite quickly, the smells took over and I began to forget my worries. Ahhh, the smells. It was quite wonderful to explore the local common. I could smell dogs, lots of them; rabbits, hundreds of them but all hidden away; squirrels everywhere but none to be seen; horses, birds, plants and, of course, humans. To say that I was intoxicated would be an understatement. Although the smells in Thailand had been more vibrant, I had not been in a free space for almost two years and, boy, was it exciting!

I don't know how long we were out, but I must have been away with the fairies as, all of a sudden, I found myself facing two humans just a few metres away. This really scared me as I hadn't noticed them approaching. "Oh my God", said one of them to my human; "Whatever happened to your dog, it's covered in scars?". This was a question that I was to hear time and time again over the coming months. Initially Mr Blue excused himself saying that I was a very timid dog but in time, as I became more relaxed with humans, he would explain how I was found impaled on an iron rod in a disused building in Thailand ... and I could see these humans look on in horror as he told them my back-story. It encouraged me that these people were visibly upset to hear what had happened to me because it meant that they cared for animals and their welfare.

My human would go on to tell them all about Soi Dog and then about the dog meat trade; and often they would interject, saying, "Stop. We don't want to know any more". This always frustrated my human who would then mutter to himself something along the lines of; for evil to prevail, all it takes is for good men to stand still; as we marched off into the distance!

Chapter 25

The dog meat trade

Although I was not a victim of the dog meat trade, I soon discovered that my human was very involved in fighting this horribly evil trade and that, after his first visit to Soi Dog, he had founded an organisation called Stop Eating Dogs.

Although, by nature, I am a gentle soul, I get very distressed and angry when I think about what we dogs call the Trade of Shame. You humans call we dogs Man's Best Friend and yet you allow nations to not only eat us, but also to torture us first. It is known around the world that people do this, the internet is full of unpalatable stories, photographs and videos, and yet the majority of humans turn a blind eye to these appalling atrocities. My own human has told me, time and time again, that people who have asked him about his work with dogs then stop him mid-reply saying they simply can't bear to listen to any more.

The trouble is, if people don't listen, or worse still if they feign ignorance, then nothing happens and us dogs (and cats) continue to be violently abused and brutally killed.

In writing this chapter I want to thank my A3 friend Fendi and my Uncle Boonrod for their help, as both are dog meat trade survivors. Uncle Boonrod isn't really my uncle (we street dogs don't know our lineage!) but he is a Soi Dog hero and I would feel a bit embarrassed and over familiar calling him Boonrod. It's different with Fendi as we became such very good friends while I lived at Soi Dog and she personally told me of her rescue that fateful night on the banks of the Mekong River.

The killing and eating of dogs and cats is illegal in Thailand, but that doesn't stop rogue traders from rounding up street dogs and stealing pet dogs and cats and trucking them off to Vietnam, via Laos. The dog meat trade is prevalent in China, South Korea, the Philippines, Laos, Vietnam, Cambodia and the region of Nagaland in India. It is estimated that up to 30 million dogs are killed every year for human consumption; that's a staggering 80,000 dogs a day. It makes me shiver just to think of it ...

In South Korea dog meat dishes are so common they have their own name - Gaegogi. Dogs are farmed in hideously cruel conditions in thousands of dog meat farms. These poor dogs, some bred on the farms, the majority stolen from the streets, are kept in small cages and never get to feel the ground under their feet. They are fed slop, a mix of waste food, minced dead dog, rice and water and, in many cases, do not even have access to a separate bowl of clean drinking water. Many of these dogs are ridden with disease which, cruelty aside, is a very good reason to stop farming dogs and then eating them.

In Vietnam, Laos, Cambodia and China dogs are not farmed but are subjected to hideous cruelty none the less. In these countries, vast numbers of street dogs and family pets are stolen off the streets (pet dogs are not confined to homes and gardens as they are here in England) and then sold at meat markets. In China alone, 20 million dogs suffer this fate.

Still to this day dogs endure horrific, slow deaths as many Asians mistakenly believe that the release of adrenaline (caused by terror and pain) enhances the taste and "healing properties" of dog meat. In Vietnam, rogue traders forcibly pump water into dogs (by inserting pipes down their throats or up their back passages) to increase their weight, thereby adding to their market value. This everyday practice is excruciatingly painful and can destroy our organs. Many dogs die in this process.

Across various parts of Asia they hang dogs by their necks and beat them with sticks (to "tenderise" the meat). Many thousands of dogs are blow-torched while alive, or skinned while alive, or boiled while alive. They have limbs hacked off, they are electrocuted and they are bludgeoned to death. To prevent them screaming in agony and fear, their muzzles are taped or wired shut.

The lucky ones are simply drowned in cages. Ten dogs to a cage. Utterly horrific but quicker than most of the alternatives.

I've mentioned elsewhere the hideous crates that are used to ship hundreds and often thousands of dogs at a time to illegal slaughter houses; and I've heard first hand from my friend Fendi the horror of such a journey in such a crate.

Both Uncle Boonrod and Fendi were rescued by a team from Soi Dog working alongside the Royal Thai Police and I feel it is important to stress there that there are millions of good people in Asia who abhor the dog meat trade. There are many thousands of Asian animal activists who often risk severe retribution by intercepting trucks loaded with dogs on their way to slaughter. The current President of South Korea claims to be a dog lover and hopefully he will, sooner rather than later, shut down his country's pre-historic and abhorrently cruel dog meat farms. China has passed laws stating that it is illegal to kill cats and dogs for the purpose of selling their meat, although these laws are rarely enforced.

Thankfully, in addition to all its work with Thai rescue dogs such as myself, Soi Dog is working with schools across Asia, introducing young Asians to the joys of pet dogs and cats. Indeed, many young Asian families now keep dogs and cats as pets which is wonderful news.

People reading my tale who are unfamiliar with the dog and

cat meat trade might find this chapter as hard to believe as it is to read. If in any doubt as to the authenticity of my story, please research "the Asian dog meat trade" on what you humans call the internet and see for yourself what is happening today, and every day, across Asia.

Culture Vs torture

As an aside, one of my human's neighbours once berated him for interfering with what he called national culture, but when and where was it cultural to torture animals before killing them? Yes, humans have eaten dogs over the years but white humans also used to enslave black humans and adult humans used to make child humans work in mines. It could be argued that these shocking, evil crimes were also cultural, but culture should never be used as an excuse for cruelty.

Take China for example, the largest dog eating nation in the world:-

Puyi was the 12th and final Emperor of the Qing dynasty, China's last imperial dynasty. Puyi and his wife, the Empress Wanrong, were dog lovers; indeed their house was full of dogs!

We know that dogs were revered by the Manchu rulers of China. This stemmed from the legend of the first Manchu leader, Nurhachi, whose life was saved by a dog. It should be no surprise, therefore, to learn that for hundreds of years it was illegal to kill and consume dogs in China. Yes, villagers did eat dogs but dog meat was not an industry as it is today and dogs were respected.

This all changed in 1912 when the Kuomintang Nationalist Party took power. As a symbol of their hatred towards the Manchu, they would boil dogs alive, just to spite them.

Tragically this was only the beginning of dogs' descent into hell in China, for when the communists took power a few decades later, Chairman Mao ordered the mass execution of dogs, declaring them filthy, unclean and representative of the elite.

Does this sound like culture to you? There is no country in the world that includes torture in its culture. The horrific treatment of dogs in China is (in historical terms) a relatively new phenomenon, brought about by evil, spiteful minds.

Happily for we dogs, China is turning the corner, albeit slowly. Today the vast majority of Chinese do not eat dogs, indeed millions now keep dogs and cats as pets. But it will be many years before we dogs ever feel safe in China.

Some people abhor animal cruelty and voice their opinions, while others just accept it, often using ignorance as their excuse. These people don't want to know the truth, whether we are talking about the dog meat trade in Asia or factory farming around the world, which my two-legs tells me is equally inhumane.

FACT: If people were killed at the same rate that people slaughter animals, the whole human race would be extinct in just 17 days. It's a sobering thought ...

As a Man's Best Friend, I beg all you humans out there to do everything you can to bring the dog meat trade, indeed all animal cruelty, to an end as soon as possible.

"Cruelty and abuse are terrible monsters that hide around every corner."

John Dalley MBE
President, Soi Dog Foundation

At long last I get to meet
Mr Blue. For me, it was
love at first sight

Elle enjoying some Soi love

Khun Mo, my carer

Walking with Mr Blue

Get me out of here!

Chillin' on my sala

Soi Nopparat and I caught discussing our escape plan!

With my dear friend Yanisa

Tini, one of my lovely A3 walkers

I have a very distinctive tongue!

Getting ready for a walk with Tom

My wounds are nicely healed here

Elle sent this photo to Mr Blue after he had returned to England. I was missing him dreadfully and didn't understand why he had gone

Being measured for
my travel crate

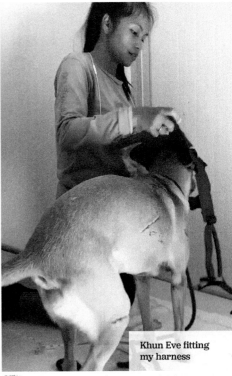

Khun Eve fitting
my harness

Eve encouraging me
to relax in my crate

The start of a VERY
long journey

AWB NO....157-2683-0300...TO...LHR

SHIPPER: MR.ROHUN CORIN BEVEN
1878 MOO 4, SOI MAIKHAO 10
MAIKHAO THALANG PHUKET 831 10
THAILAND TEL: +987262004
E-mail:ROHUN@SOIDOG.ORG

CONSIGNEE: MR.ROHUN CORIN BEVAN
C/O PBS INTERNATIONAL FREIGHT LTD
23 AIRLINKS INDUSTRIAL ESTATE
SPITFIRE WAY HOUNSLOW UK TW5 9NR
TEL:07437583297,+44777 4155244

BREED: MIXED
NAME: KNIGHT/MALE/CREAM/OCT 08, 2015
*MICROCHIP NO. 900 079 000 591 317
CONTACT 24 HOURS. NO. : +447774155244
keep in temperature 24-26.C

FEEDING AND WATERING GUIDE

To whom it may concern
**PET does not normally require additional feeding
during first 12 hours by the time of dispatch.
(05/08/2020 time 03.00 PM local time)**
-Next feeding time-
Food: (Provide) AUG 06 2020   03.00 AM
Water: (Provide) AUG 06 2020   03.00 AM

Thanks for your kindly attention and cooperative.
KEEP IN TEMPERATURE 24-26.C

LIVE ANIMAL
That's me!

My waybill come Feeding
and Watering Guide

Your Pups!

QR837/QTR837
Qatar Airways

BKK — DOH
BANGKOK   DOHA

CALIBRATED ALT. 36,000 ft
GROUND SPEED 487 kts

Departed 01:39 ago   Arriving in 04:19

Boeing 777-3DZ(ER)   REG: A7-BEB

Being loaded on board

I'm on my way
to England

Holden, Alleye, Princess Daphne, myself and Simba in Mr Blue's living room

Mr Blue tells me not to pee in his house

Freedom at last but all I want to do is sleep!

We spent the first week in our little den, far away from everyone

At first Mr Blue had to carry me everywhere

Snoozing in the hallway

My first proper walk in England. I stopped every few seconds to check that Mr Blue was still with me!

Clockwise from above:

My new limo, it is very comfortable!
On my way to work. Inspecting Mr
Blue's first Stop Eating Dogs banner

HELL ON EARTH.

One of the thousands of dog meat farms in South Korea. None of these dogs will ever see the light of day, the puppies will never get to play. Death awaits them all

이곳에선 온갖 종류의 개들

'도살'을 기다린

PHOTOS: Kara and HSI

Muzzles bound so that they cannot bite

This sweet pup has shut down

An over-bred mother

Cats share the same fate

Awaiting slaughter

Melissa in Princess Daphne's crate!

Relaxing with Françoise

Caroline was the first to call me Wagalot!

Walking with Celia

Meeting Soi Dog Pepper
(née Brianna)

My mate Rocky
in all his glory

#whosthedaddy
Myself and Soi Dog Sosay

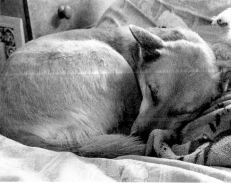

Every hour, a dog is killed because people still buy dogs from breeders instead of adopting from a shelter.

#adoptdontshop
Save a dog's life

DID YOU KNOW?

One female dog can produce **two** litters of **6-10** puppies **every year.** This means one un-spayed female and her offspring can produce **67,000** dogs in **6 years**.

An estimated 80% of the dogs in shelters will be euthanised!

WHY SPAY?
Do you know 67,000 people who want a new dog?

Absorbing my new environment
from various vantage points

With Mr Blue
on the beach

My first birthday in England and presents galore!

I see my pug
friends most days

A cuddle
from Curvy!

Plan B!
Me and Vicky

With my best
friend Daisy

Peace at last 💙

www.soidog.org

Gill Dalley
Soi Dog co-founder

1959 - 2017

All beings tremble before violence.

All love life. All fear death.

See yourself in others.

Then whom can you hurt?

What harm can you do?

Buddha

Chapter 26

Going to work

Back home in England, many thousands of miles away from the evil dog meat trade, I had come to understand that Covid was all around the world and not just in Thailand; which was why my human had been able to spend so much time with me over the past few weeks. Like many in England, Mr Blue had been told to work from home if possible but this had proved to be unsatisfactory, so now we were both going to work!

Needless to say, I had no understanding of what "going to work" meant but my human didn't seem too fussed, so I knew that it was going to be safe. After travelling to England, being reunited with Mr Blue, learning to live in his home, going for walks and meeting new humans and dogs on these walks, I wasn't sure that I was quite ready for a new adventure, but my human explained that we had no option and that going to work was going to become a part of my new life. "The honeymoon's over Knighty Knight", he joked "And now you've got to earn your keep as Chief Security Officer at Shell-Clad HQ!". He seemed to think that this was quite funny, so I wagged my tail in support and waited to see what would happen.

On Monday morning we were woken up early by a beep beep beep noise that I hadn't heard before, upon which Mr Blue bounced out of bed as if his life depended on it. Hmmm, I thought to myself, this must be work then! Much to my relief, my first day at work started with a walk and, I am sure, this walk lasted longer than our usual dawn walks. "A longer walk than normal this morning Knighty" said Mr Blue "as we won't get out for a proper walk again until much, much later, I am afraid". Breakfast followed next and, just as I was beginning to think that working life was okay, Mr Blue said "And now I want you to be a VERY brave boy".

The great joy, and to be honest at times frustration, of being a dog is that we have absolutely no idea what our humans are saying to us. We can generally pick up on the vibe; a gentle voice, an encouraging voice, an urgent voice, an angry voice; but the words themselves are meaningless; so "VERY brave" was just a noise to me and it didn't trigger any warning bells within me.

Even when my human re-fitted my harness, mindful that we had just been out for a walk, I didn't think much of it and, when we left his home, I assumed that we were simply going for another walk. Maybe when he said we had to go to work, he meant we had to go to walk, I thought but suddenly I found myself facing a van and my human was opening the doors! I had seen vans before, on the roads of Phuket, but all I knew was that vans were to be avoided as they moved very fast and were very solid and if they hit you, as they had many dogs I had met, you were in big trouble.

That said, my human was encouraging me to get INTO this van. Strangely it smelt of a mix of me and Mr Blue and it had a whole sausage in it and, before I knew what I was doing, I found myself in the van, munching on the sausage. "Well done Knighty" said Mr Blue as he closed the doors and jumped in himself. I looked around; the back of the van was big and cavernous and at the front there was one seat (occupied by my human) and a sitting space about my size. As much as I wanted to explore further, I realised that my harness was tethered to the van and that my movements were quite restricted. In the past this would have frightened me, but I was beginning to understand that anything and everything connected to

Mr Blue worked out well for me, so I manoeuvred myself into the space beside his seat and waited to see what would happen next!

Well I wasn't expecting the van to purr like a cat, but that's what it seemed to do next! My human was looking at me and asking me how I felt, but I felt fine and wagged my tail to show that I was okay. Then the van moved! Now that was a shock, but it moved slowly, so I adjusted my balance and waited to see what would happen next. Because of my accident, my legs are not as strong as most dogs', but of course Mr Blue knew this so he was driving very smoothly. After what seemed like the length of a walk, throughout which I swayed left and right, and backwards and forwards, but never fell over, we arrived at a big building. On the outside were two square signs; one said Shell-Clad and the other said Stop Eating Dogs; and this, announced Mr Blue, was work! To be honest, I was expecting something completely different and, to be fair, when we went inside it was quite different! There were no sofas to sit on, no beds to hide under and the whole room, which was huge, looked a bit like a bigger version of my bolt-hole back home, ie the study. There were lots of desks and chairs and not much else. I didn't much like it at home when Mr Blue went to his desk, as he seemed to forget me for a while as he stared at a small screen and tapped his fingers on a plate in front of the screen; and I realised with something of a sinking feeling that this was "work" as he called it.

Up to this stage I had had my human's attention 24 hrs a day and I had got very used to it. I had almost forgotten that I used to live in fear of humans and that I used to avoid them all the time. My new life with Mr Blue was perfect and consisted of walking, eating and sleeping and a few games; although I didn't really understand these and was struggling to participate as I suspect was expected of me! Now, at work, I realised that Mr Blue had other priorities and that I had to lie low and wait until work was over. That said, I was taken out for a "lap of the block" every two hours or so although, at the time of writing, we have yet to complete a full lap of the block as I always lose my nerve half way around!

I didn't particularly like work but my human kept stressing how important my job was and that with me on site, no one was ever going to "raid" the office. This gave me purpose although, to be honest, I spent most of my time sleeping under Mr Blue's desk. I knew from other dogs that I had met, that many of them were left at home all day long while their humans went to work, so I knew that I was one of the lucky ones, but I still craved the weekends; two days a week when, once again, I became my human's priority.

One day Mr Blue said to me "Duncan's coming in tomorrow. You'll like him, he is the most decent man I know." He went on to tell me that Duncan was his No 2 and that they had been working together for many years, but what he didn't tell me was that Duncan was a cat lover and that he didn't much like dogs. It's a funny thing, but we dogs just know when people are not dog lovers, even when they are kind to us and/or keep out of our way. As hard as I tried to be brave, Duncan frightened me from the outset and I found myself spending more and more time under my human's desk. Duncan never threatened me, actually he was something of a gentle giant and he often left treats out for me, but he smelt of a strange mix of cat and chinchilla and that totally spooked me. To this day, I avoid Duncan at work and I always make sure that I am as far away from him as possible. I don't know why he frightens me and I certainly can't explain it; and even though I know that he would never hurt me, I also know that we will never be friends. I wish that I could feel more relaxed with him as my human thinks so highly of him, but some things are just not to be.

Truth told, I don't much like "work" as I get very bored, and I get the impression that my human feels the same. The intensity and solitude of Covid life seems to have hit him hard and only very occasionally do I see the relaxed and supremely happy man that I first met at Soi Dog last Christmas.

Chapter 27

Meeting Mr Blue's family and friends

Work aside, I was becoming quite comfortable with my new life in England. First and foremost, and most importantly, there was my very own two-legs, Mr Blue, and with him came love, comfort, safety, warmth, food and an all-round cosy feeling. My human really understands me and my underlying fears and, as a result, he protects me at all times. Initially our home was a no-go zone to all and sundry but, as weeks passed by, we started to receive a few carefully selected visitors.

The first of these were his sons, William and Jack. They were both bigger, younger and stronger than Mr Blue and, needless to say, they frightened me for no reason other than they were unknown quantities, so I hid in the study during their visit. Over time I have got to know them a little bit better, but I am still uncomfortable in their presence. It's not so bad when we are outside walking but when we are in the house, I tend to keep my distance. I know that Mr Blue would love me to bound up to them and bark Hello whenever they arrive and, hopefully, one day I will. In reality, we dogs do not understand "family" and, as far as I am concerned, William and Jack are two more humans, tall humans at that, and humans frighten me.

The next to visit was Melissa who I had met briefly at Soi Dog. Melissa had been my human's walking partner on his first visit in

2018 and they have a rather special friendship as a result. Happily for me, Melissa is quite petite and fitted very comfortably in Princess Daphne's travel crate which I found most encouraging! That said, Melissa arrived with her dad Mick and, as hard as I tried to be brave, once again I found myself retreating into the study, although I did (under my human's guidance) allow them both to sit with me for photos! On another day I met Melissa's mum, Celia, who I knew quite well from Soi Dog as she had walked me regularly. Despite knowing her well, and despite my human showing me a video of Celia walking with me in the Gill Dalley Sanctuary the evening before she arrived, I still found myself hiding in the study throughout her visit ... until we went out for a walk that is!

One day my human said; "We have a very special visitor this afternoon, Knighty. She is called Françoise and she was Kimba's best friend".

By way of reminder, Kimba was my human's previous, and very much loved, rescue dog, in whose pawprints I was doing my very best to follow. The thought of meeting Kimba's best friend filled me with dread but, the minute I saw Françoise, all my fears faded and for the first time ever, I felt no urge to bolt and hide in the study. "Bonjour adorable voyageur, tu es trop mignon et nous allons être copains." she said to me in a gentle voice, with an accent that was very different to anything I had heard previously. Before I knew it, I was sitting on the floor beside her and she was stroking me. Mr Blue was bowled over, indeed he could hardly believe what he was seeing with his own eyes. "Well well, Mr Knight", he teased, "So you're not really terrified of all humans after all, are you?!".

Other visitors came and went and, slowly, I began to grow bolder. By that I mean that I would still hide in the study, but every now and again I would creep along the hallway and poke my snout into the living room. If people ignored me I would sometimes take a couple of paces into the room but as soon as they said hello or made eye contact with me, I was off again!

Mr Blue's mother, Sheelagh, came to lunch every Saturday and, by around the tenth week, I had summoned up sufficient courage to join them in the lounge for pre-lunch aperitifs (a word that Françoise taught me). This ritual was always accompanied by the munching of nuts and raisins and, much to my amazement, I discovered that if I looked at my human for long enough, and lovingly enough, a few nuts would somehow find their way into my mouth. Yes, I was learning the tricks of the (being a pet) trade and I was coming to understand that it was actually quite easy to manipulate my human; although I vowed never to take (serious) advantage of this situation! These nuts he gave me, incidentally, were always unsalted cashew nuts; and he never gave me any raisins, explaining that these were bad for me.

One Saturday Mr Blue spent an inordinately long time tidying up his house. I've always enjoyed watching him move around but I found today a bit unsettling. Firstly he was using a machine that rolled up and down the floor making a strange sucking noise and also he was spraying surfaces and wiping them with cloths. I didn't much like the artificial smells and the sucking noise unnerved me so I retired to the study (where I still had a spare bed). After a while my human came to find me and apologised for the noise (interestingly, he never apologised for the smell, it was almost as if it didn't hit him SMACK on the nose). Then he said "Tomorrow my family is coming for lunch Knighty. There will be my Ma and William and Jack, all of whom you have met before; and also my daughter Scarlett and Toby and Rocky who you have never met". Not knowing what he was saying and not understanding what any of this meant, but noticing that the sucking noises had stopped and that the chemical smells had faded slightly, I wagged my tail and accompanied him back into the lounge.

Come Sunday morning Mr Blue was buzzing and clearly very excited. "Remember my family is coming to visit today Knighty Knight and, while you might find it all a little bit overpowering, it will be a good test of your resolve my friend."

I hope he doesn't forget to walk me, I thought to myself as I munched through my breakfast. I knew he was excited and I feared that he might possibly overlook our morning routine as he pottered around the house tidying things up. Just as I was thinking the worst he piped up; "Right, it's time for our walk Mr Knight. We'll make it a long one as we might not get out again until after lunch".

In time the door bell rang and my human's Ma arrived. I knew her well and was glad to see her although, of course, I kept my distance as I always do. Ma human was followed by William and Jack who still unnerved me but knowing this, they had kindly brought me a feeding toy, and anything to do with food is always welcome in my mind.

Finally the door bell rang a third time. This is it, I thought to myself, these are the ones that I have never met ... be brave and hold your ground ... if you can.

The door opened and I was confronted by a big tall man and next to him a rather petite two-legs. This must be Toby and Scarlett I thought to myself, wondering who and where Rocky might be. Just as I pondered this there was a flash of movement at ground level and the most extra-ordinary looking creature I have ever seen rushed into the room and bounded up on to the sofa. He/she/it (?) was very short and rather round and, although he/she/it smelt like a dog, he/she/it had a pig's curly tail and no snout to speak of!

"Hello" said the creature, "my name is Rocky and I'm a pug. You must be Mr Knight, I've heard all about you from my humans".

"What sort of animal is a pug?" I asked politely, only for Rocky to roll about laughing. "I'm a dog of course, silly" said Rocky "what did you think I was?"

"Surely not? No, you can't possibly be a dog!" I replied, not intending to be rude, but I was just so surprised. I had met hundreds of dogs in my life, but never one that looked even remotely like Rocky. Happily I needn't have worried about offending him as he was, I soon discovered, the happiest dog I had ever met. Although my nervousness necessitated me retiring to my study at about this time, I repeatedly popped my head around the corner throughout the visit to watch this strange creature in wonderment. He spent the whole time bouncing from one human's lap to the next, completely without fear, soaking up their love and affection. I had never seen anything remotely like it!

The only slight downer to this extraordinary Rocky experience occurred during our afternoon walk. Although Rocky raced around like a mad, demented rabbit, I noticed that he was constantly out of breath and at times gasping. Rocky explained to me that humans had made him the way he was by selecting only the shortest of snouted dogs for breeding. By doing this over many years, humans created "pugs", dogs without snouts that would spend much of their lives struggling for breath. Rocky went on to say that short snout and snoutless dogs were officially known as 'brachycephalic breeds' because they suffered from Brachycephalic Obstructive Airway Syndrome. As well as restricting breathing, BOAS also affects a dog's ability to exercise, thermo-regulate, sleep, play and undertake other normal behaviours.

Not for the first time I wondered to myself how humans had become the dominant species on earth as they did so many stupid things. "I'd love to be able to breathe freely like you" Rocky croaked, "but every day I have to be careful not to over do it." Then he perked up: "Mind you, I'm the happiest dog" he said (stating the obvious), "I live with Toby and Scarlett and so my life is just perfect".

Poor Rocky. I had always taken breathing for granted and I found myself overwhelmed and very much in awe of this amazing little dog that was so happy and so determined to enjoy every single moment of his life, despite the obstacles thrown at him by selfish dog breeders.

A few months later, just before Christmas, Toby and Scarlett got married. I wasn't invited as Covid restricted the guest list to just eight two-legs, but Rocky donned his smartest jacket and a top hat and snuck in under the radar; aka under the security guard's line of sight. I've never been to a wedding and doubt I ever will, but I am absolutely sure that Rocky was in his element ... without doubt he would have been the pawfect wedding guest!

Chapter 28

Humans Vs dogs

When my human wakes up, very often the first words he says to me are "Good morning little man, how did you sleep last night?" and I sit there thinking to myself - Surely by now he MUST know that I am a dog? He's a funny fellow my human, I can't quite work him out!

All of which raises the question of communication between humans and dogs, dogs and humans and dogs and dogs.

I admire much about my human's form. I think it is very clever that he can stand on two paws and his hand-paws look very useful indeed. Sometimes I wish that I was the same, but then I see my human fall over on a walk and I think to myself, four paws is good! I don't think I would like to have to dress every morning and undress at night ... and make my bed; we dogs just curl up as and when (and where) it suits us! The one thing that I really do like about my human is that he has the advantage of speech. Humans can talk to each other in enormous detail using hundreds of different words, not that I understand any of them yet, with the possible exception of WAIT which is a bit of a work-in-progress! They can tell stories, they can explain situations and events to each other and they can even teach each other complicated things, like how to change a set of brake pads on a Ford Fusion. I know this as

I saw my human teach someone how to do this just recently.

The trouble is, far too many humans think (maybe in the moment) that we dogs understand their language ... which we most certainly do not. There is absolutely no point in telling us "How many times do I have to tell you not to bark at the postman?" as we have absolutely no idea what you are talking about. Anyhow, surely the purpose of a postman is to be barked at! If you are a clever human you will have taught us a few basic words such as STOP or SIT but even these words need to be said with the same tone of voice every time. STOP said in a level tone and supported by a simple hand signal has a completely different meaning to STOOOP! shouted at the top of your voice while accompanied by a waving fist. Surely you humans must understand this? Don't scream and shout at us if we have done something "wrong" as in something you do not like. For starters we probably don't know exactly what we have done wrong and secondly, we don't understand what (or why) you are shouting at us. I cannot begin to explain how unsettling this is, being shouted at by humans, and not knowing what you have done wrong (usually something done a while earlier and long since lost in our memories). I was always being shouted at on the streets in Thailand and having things thrown at me but, happily my human hasn't shouted at me (yet). Not even once! That said, I have met dogs in England who live in fear of upsetting their humans and have even been punished without having any idea of what they have done wrong. If only there was some way of us asking "What I have done to upset you?" but we can't, so please be patient with us.

While on the subject of language, can anyone explain the following to me as it is possibly the biggest mystery in my new life. Every day, at some stage, my human will look at his watch and say, "Hey, it's Knight time!" immediately after which he will play with me and/or take me out for a lovely long walk. But sometimes when he looks at his watch and says, "Hey, it's night time" he goes upstairs, climbs into bed and goes to sleep! Leaving me downstairs chasing my tail and wondering when the fun is going to begin! Understanding you humans really is very confusing ...

In addition to language, you humans have excellent eyesight and the benefit of full colour vision! Every day in your life is the equivalent of seeing a film in IMAX but I get the impression that you don't fully appreciate this wonder, which is a shame as the world around you smells quite extraordinary and, I am sure, must look utterly breathtaking.

We dogs don't have such great eyesight. For a start everything that we see, we see from sub-knee level, well I certainly do! So a small shrub or a coffee table, which you might hardly notice, can be a mountain to us, an obstacle that we cannot see around or over! Seeing everything from knee height is very, very different, I can assure you. If in doubt, get down on all fours yourself, as my humans does so often on walks, and see your world from our pawspective. Even if we could view the world from your height, what we would see would be very different. For a start, our colour spectrum is quite limited compared to humans, but we are not colour blind as some people think. The colours we notice the most are blues and greeny-yellows, other colours are not as powerful to we dogs. I suspect that midday colour to us is not dissimilar to dusk colour to you, in that you can still see but the colours are muted. Another consideration is that your eyes are in the front of your heads and ours are off-set, one on each side. This gives us a great width of vision, 250° to 270° generally, but it also means that sometimes we don't notice things right in front of our noses, unless they smell of course! My mate Rocky the pug is an exception as there are always exceptions to the rule, even in dog world! Rocky's head is a bit more human in shape than mine as he has no snout to bark of, so his vision is different. Rocky is always teasing me that pugs are more advanced than us street dogs and that, one day, his breed will just stand up on two legs and start walking the walk. I love Rocky, he's one of my best friends, but I think he is a bit barking mad to be honest.

Anyhow, back to what we dogs can and can't see. Here lies the greatest difference between me and my human; for while he sees the world, I smell the world.

Make no mistake, what we dogs lack in vision we make up for in smelling! In short we have quite MAGNIFICENT olfactory senses; yes, our sense of smell is brilliant. As I write these words my human is reading a wonderful book called Inside of a Dog by Alexandra Horowitz and he has just told me that, while a human nose might have up to six million receptors, a dog's nose can have as many as 300 million! Apparently we dogs can even smell one spoonful of sugar mixed into one million gallons of water. To be honest I have never tried this, but I find it quite amazing! I think it is fair to say that our sense of smell is nothing to be sniffed at!

You humans might walk into a room and think "Oh, it's a bit stuffy, I need to open a window" while we dogs, in the same room at the same time, would think: "Hmmm, I like the smell of yesterday's meal; my human was in here a few minutes ago and he wasn't wearing shoes; those flowers he threw out last week still reek; I can smell the three friends he had over last night; that new rug smells a bit moth-bally to me; someone has sat on my half of the sofa and has been reading a newspaper; my human had toast this morning (and burnt it); I can smell car fumes, the windows must be open ... hmmm, it's time to go as I can smell chicken and my human is a vegan, so that means he is preparing my breakfast". Yes, we can quite literally smell and interpret all of that and very much more, albeit we cannot explain what we can smell in the Queen's English, nor anyone's English for that matter!

Our world is all about smell. We know if a petal has just been pollinated by a bee, we can smell the difference between a whole leaf and a torn leaf (how can you humans not smell that?); indeed everywhere we go is just crammed full of smells. As much as I love my human I have noticed that he says things like "Hmmm, that smells nice" (usually food) or "Yuk, what's that horrible smell?" (usually something old in the fridge). Never does he comment on anything in between. Sometimes, during a walk, I am jumping up and down with excitement as I can smell so many different things and all he says is: "Are you enjoying your walk, old boy?".

So we dogs see the world, or rather smell it, from a very, very different perspective to humans! Although we get excited by different things and can't actually talk to you, we can communicate this excitement with you as every dog owner knows!

On the subject of communication, I'd like to clarify a point; the kick-back myth. Most humans are convinced that we pee constantly to claim a particular territory as our own. This is so wrong! Yes, in Thailand we hung around in packs and did our best to avoid other dogs' territories but, in the main, our peeing is more about leaving our 'calling card' for other dogs to pick up on and notice. To us a lamp post or a tree or a car wheel is like a noticeboard onto which we feel a huge urge to leave our scent so that other dogs can get to understand and know us, even before they meet us. The kick-back myth? We are not hiding or disguising our scent, we are enhancing it as we have glands in our paws that ADD to our scent!

All of which brings me on to another major human Vs dog issue - bottoms! Please don't stop us smelling each other's bottoms as this is really important to us. I know that you humans find it a little embarrassing and, although I find it hard to believe, my own human assures me that it is not a practice that you humans undertake. But for us dogs, bottom smelling is as natural as you humans making eye contact while talking. We learn so much from smelling each other's bottoms, we really do. Please try to remember that our primary means of communication and of understanding the world around us is smell ... without smell we are lost souls.

To illustrate this point, I can think of no better example than during my last Christmas at Soi Dog in Phuket. There were a couple of (well meaning I am sure) volunteers whose full time job was to train dogs, specifically gun dogs. This couple believed that dogs had to be 100% under the control of the humans walking them at all times and one of their ways of enforcing this was to not allow we dogs to stop and sniff during walks. The commotion this caused in the runs, no one wanted to walk with them! In those days we only got 20 minutes a day to walk and those 20 minutes were the highlight of our day. Imagine not being allowed to sniff ... it would be like we dogs taking you humans to visit the Seven Wonders of the World and making you wear blindfolds throughout. Seriously, that is the equivalent of us walking and not being allowed to sniff...

Our walks with you two-legs are our greatest pleasure in life, it's what we look forward to all day and every day. Please be patient and let us sniff as much as we want to!

Chapter 29

Designer dogs

As I have alluded to elsewhere in my story, there are an estimated 600,000,000 stray dogs in the world today. Another estimate, equally frightening, is that as many as 5,000 healthy dogs are destroyed (as in killed) every day in shelters around the world.

Which begs the question, why do humans continue to breed dogs at such a rate and even create new dog "breeds" known as designer dogs? And I thought we dogs owned the title "barking mad"!

Don't get me wrong, I have nothing against these dogs, it's the humans who are at fault as we do not need more dogs in the world. Surely 600,000,000 stray dogs is proof enough of that?

A man by the name of Wally Coonron is credited with creating the world's first designer dog, the labradoodle. At the time, even he said; "I've created a Frankenstein's monster". I don't think he meant that his labradoodle was a monster, rather the concept of what he had done was somewhat monstrous.

At the end of the day a designer dog is a cross-breed or a hybrid, call it what you want; but it's nothing more, nothing less. In the old days cross-breeds were called 'mutts' and they were usually free to a good home. Now humans call them designer dogs and make a stupidly big fuss over their lineage. Furthermore, many unscrupulous breeders interbreed their cross-breeds to create as many puppies as possible (puppies = cash in their minds). Mating closely related dogs can and does cause all sorts of hereditary conditions such hip dysplasia, epilepsy, hypothyroidism, cancer, eye disorders and more.

Furthermore, the mother dogs are often over-bred, only to be discarded when their litters dry up. It is absolutely criminal and it should not be allowed.

My human says Adopt Don't Shop and he is right. Everyone who buys a dog indirectly contributes to a beautiful, healthy dog being destroyed in a shelter. Everyone who adopts a dog i) saves that dog's life and ii) frees up shelter space for another dog.

On my walks I regularly meet a "cockapoo" called Harry. To me he is just a dog, albeit a very nice dog; but his bum smells just like any other dog I know. Actually that's not true as we all smell a bit different, but the point I am making here is that his bum doesn't smell of roses even though he is supposedly a designer dog. My human tells me that people are paying over £2,000 for spaniel/poodle cross-breeds and calling them cockapoos instead of mutts. Why do humans fall for such hype? Is it vanity, is it ignorance or are they simply well-meaning but misinformed people? Whatever it is, nothing can justify the knock-on effects, ie thousands of shelter dogs being destroyed every single day around the world, while breeders continue to create new mutts with fancy names ... and then sell them for huge sums of money to people who want something "special".

On a less serious (but still quite impawtant) note, I was on SnoutTime the other day, chatting with my friend Sosay (#whosthedaddy) and we were laughing about these so called designer dogs.

The thing is, me and Sosay reckon that we are part dingo and part labrador, possibly with a few other breeds mixed in. In our minds that makes us Dingadors; an all-new, previously unknown and utterly unique designer dog breed of huge distinction.

My goodness, we must both be worth £$€ thousands!

Chapter 30

A very confusing week

September 2020

By now I was beginning to feel quite settled. I lived in a nice big house with a wonderful human and his training seemed to be going to plan. We were in a routine that worked really well for me. Human took me out for an early walk every morning and then we came home for breakfast. Depending on the day of the week, we then had a short rest (human usually read a book) after which we went on another walk or we went to work ... or rather my human did, I just tagged along for the ride! We then had lunch and, depending on whether or not we were at work, we had a mid afternoon or early evening walk. This was followed by dinner and another shorter walk before bed time (or my human called night time).

Although my human occasionally had guests, some of whose smells I recognised, I mainly had him all to myself and, thanks to some good advice from Kimba's vibes throughout the house, I had him under my paw, or so I thought!

One Saturday morning my two-legs got up extra early which should have triggered alarm bells as he is usually a bit lazy on Saturdays. He seemed a touch agitated, no maybe animated is a better word. He was clearly on edge, a cross between excited and nervous ... and he kept rushing around the house tidying up things that already looked extremely tidy to me.

I was certainly seeing a different side to Mr Blue! Previously he had always seemed rather chilled on his days off and I was intrigued by this new persona. Happily he remembered to take me out for a pre-breakfast walk ... a bit longer than usual ... and when we got home he gave me my breakfast with a little bit of extra chicken. I might only be a dog but it seemed to me that he was buttering me up for something that was about to happen ... and I had a strange feeling that he was worried that I might not approve.

My fears were heightened when I saw him get ready to go out ... without me ... which he very rarely did. "I won't be long" he said "And when I come back we are going to have so much fun together". It seemed to me that he over-emphasised the "we" but for now all I could do was settle down in the study and worry about what he may or may not have meant.

Days later, or so it seemed, I heard the key turn in the lock and the familiar words "Don't worry Knighty, it's just me" as the door opened. In a flash I was up, tail wagging with my best happy grin in place until, to my distress, I realised that there were two humans in the doorway. And one of them was a curvy two-legs ...

As I explained earlier, my human has had guests before and, under normal circumstances, an extra person would not have worried me too much. I would simply have retreated into my study, knowing that human would tell his guest not to disturb me: "Let him come to you if he wants to, but do not go to him and, if he visits us, try not to look him in the eye." I had heard this many times before but this time something was different. Human had a silly grin on his face and was clearly in a state of extreme excitement. If he had had a tail, I am sure it would have been wagging.

"On no" I thought to myself, "What is happening? Who is this curvy two-legs that my human is bringing into our house?" It just felt weird to me ... this was very different.

Strangely, curvy two-legs seemed to know me. "Hello Mr Knight" she said, "Do you remember me?" and actually I did, well certainly I remembered her smell. Brave as I am, at this stage I thought it best to retire to my study and watch developments from afar. My human continued to blunder his way through the morning: "Can I take your coat? Would you like a drink? Are you warm enough? Is that comfortable? How about something to eat?" etc. This was all well and good but, for a while, he seemed to forget my existence although, to be fair, I was happy in my hideaway.

But, of course, he hadn't forgotten me and mid-morning he offered me a walk ... or rather he said to curvy two-legs "Shall we take Mr Knight out for a walk?". Honestly, as if I couldn't answer that question for myself! Happily the walk was wonderful as my human held my leash and curvy two-legs held her distance, although I think perhaps she had something in her eyes as they kept fluttering at my human. I had seen human act a bit like this before with his children but never with an adult. I was both worried and intrigued ... and to be honest, a little bit scared.

That night, after another walk, dinner and a final short walk, I decided that I needed to work on a strategy. My plan was to wait until they were both asleep and to then have a good think but, before I could do this, I had to sit through a lot of chit-chat and giggling. Human and curvy two-legs seemed very involved with each other, although I did notice that my human kept looking at me, as if he felt a guilty about his new friend.

Eventually curvy two-legs went upstairs and my human made up his bed on the floor next to me and settled down, as he did every night. When I was sure he was asleep, I gave him a good sniffing over (always a good start when working on strategy) and he smelt different, almost as if he was wearing perfume (which I knew he didn't). "Oh no", I thought, "This is bad, what am I going to do?" Fortunately my human had, subliminally or otherwise, prepared me for this moment as, the week before, we had sat down together and watched a film called The Art of Racing in the Rain. In this beautiful film, a human very much in love with a dog, unexpectedly falls in love with a curvy two-legs and, between them, they make an all-new mini two-legs. In the film Enzo (the dog) learns to love the curvy two-legs and the all-new human every bit as much as his own human. With all of this in mind, and knowing that my human had already created not one but three all-new two-legs of his own (and was therefore unlikely to want any more), I decided to go along with him and learn to like his curvy two-legs as much as I could.

My resolve was put to the test quite severely the very next morning when my human asked: "Did you sleep well? Were you warm enough? Was your bed comfortable?" I was just about to answer "Yes thank you!" to all three questions, when he continued: "Would you like tea or coffee? Do you take sugar and milk? Are you hungry? What would you like to do today?". I looked up and there she was ... and I am ashamed to say, I almost growled. Once again my human had morphed into a puppy-eyed, floppy monster, grinning like a hungry hyena and incapable of sane, logical thought; although I would still like to think that the first three questions had been directed at me!

And so the tone of engagement was set. My human seemed smitten with curvy two-legs and she, in turn, seemed rather taken with him. Somewhere in between, I kept bobbing up and down, reminding them of my existence. To be fair to human, the week was built around me and my requirements to eat, walk, play, pee, poo and sleep (am I really that uncomplicated); but my exclusivity had been breached.

For the first time in my life I had to share my human and it wasn't easy. Curvy two-legs could do all sorts of things that I couldn't like talk and cook and sing and other things that I didn't understand ... and all I could do was look lovingly at him and beg for (more) attention. Something told me that, if the house caught fire, he would rescue me first, but I was getting worried that he might have to think about it for a while. Then I remembered that I had vowed to learn to like curvy two-legs, which was proving more difficult than I had anticipated.

Those who have got this far in my story will know that I am a shy fellow and that it is not in my nature to be up-front and overtly friendly. But for human's sake I made a BIG effort and the week passed really quickly. In curvy two-legs' defence, she made every effort to befriend me with sweet words and, more importantly, cuts of freshly cooked chicken and I began to think that this could work; perhaps we could become a chein à trois after all? Curvy (as I now thought of her) even presented my human with a beautiful drawing of me! She could have given him a self-portrait but no, that was very definitely me, and my best side too, so she was clearly making an effort. Every now and again, when human was out of earshot, she would say "Pleeaase like me Knighty" and slowly but surely I began to think that I really could.

Then suddenly she was gone. She left the house as she had arrived, side by side with my human with him carrying her case, and when he returned, he returned alone. One side of me couldn't believe my luck; I had my human all to myself again; but the other side was sad. Sad because I realised that my human was sad, and sad too because I was just beginning to almost like her. That night, when I curled up next to human on the floor of the living room, I found myself thinking ... I do hope that Curvy comes back soon.

Chapter 31

Fear of the unknown

A lone bark echos over the valley while I am taking my morning walk. My ears immediately prick up (well metaphorically at least, as my ears are always up) and I become intensely alert. Was it the bark of a dog asking to be allowed back indoors after a morning pee, or was it the bark of a dog or dogs tracking me from afar? I have no way of knowing but, for the rest of my walk, I constantly cast backward glances to ensure that I am not being stalked. It is the same when we pass humans and other dogs on walks, I keep them in my sight until they are out of sight, as it were. Other than when indoors with my human, I am never totally relaxed. It's the curse of us soi/street dogs; we were all brought up in a world where letting your guard down could cost you a meal or, in extreme circumstances, your life.

I know that my fear of humans must seem irrational to many, especially as I now live in a country of self-proclaimed animal lovers, but you have to consider my background.

I come from a continent where an average of 80,000 dogs a DAY are slaughtered for their meat. Where people skin animals alive (cattle, dogs, cats etc) without thinking anything of it; where people set up traps for dogs; where people attack dogs with machetes or purposefully run them over; where people shoot dogs with bows and arrows; where people welcome small puppies into their homes only to abandon them when they grow up and lose their cuteness; where people kick dogs, throw stones at them and beat them. Please understand, being a dog in Asia is nothing at all like being a dog in England. I used to spend 24 hrs a day on edge, stressed and wound up like a spring, never knowing what was around the corner, what harm might befall me.

This is why I am such a nervous dog. I have heard so many people berate my human for "over protecting" me, that I feel I have to try and explain why I will never ever become an everyday pet dog, however much socialising I now do.

Since arriving in England I have met quite a few puppies on my walks, and at first I was amazed to see how comfortable they were in such close proximity to humans. I have since discovered that this is because their humans take them to 'socialisation' classes from a very early age. At these classes they learn to relax in the presence of other humans and, just as impawtantly, alongside all the other dogs.

Although I have never been to one of these classes, I think it highly unlikely that the humans throw stones at the pups or chase them with machetes, threatening to kill them. Nor, I suspect, do the dogs have to fight each other over whatever treats are being offered during training. The fact is, these pups are much loved by their humans and are fed regularly, so they are not living in fear of their lives while being hungry all the time.

Now compare this to my early life, where every human was a potential threat to my very existence, even child humans. I spent three years dodging humans all day and every day, from the moment I was born up until my entrapment in Soi Thummasopa. It's also worth remembering that at three years old, we dogs are fully functioning adults so, in my case, the whole of my childhood and teenage years were lived in fear of my life. Even now, a few months into my new life in England, strangers really frighten me and I am quite sure they always will. It's not a question of being brave or otherwise ... but rather I know how dangerous and violent humans can be!

A while ago I was in the kitchen with Mr Blue when suddenly, without warning, I heard another male voice speaking right behind me. I spun around in a panic, but no one was there. Or rather, someone had to be there as someone was talking but I couldn't smell anyone, which meant that no one was there. This utterly spooked me as you can imagine, and I started to shake violently. I must have whined too as my human looked down in alarm. His arm moved and suddenly the talking stopped; but my shaking didn't. An invisible man had snuck up on me without me knowing ... can you imagine anything more terrifying to a street dog trying to come to terms with humans? In time I came to understand that my human had a box that talked and sometimes played music. How it does this I don't know, but I still find his radio extremely unnerving.

Fortunately my human understood my distress, as something similar had once happened to his son William. Mr Blue explained that, many years ago, they had moved into a house next door to a farm. William, who was very young at the time, had been playing in the garden next to the fence when, suddenly, he was punched very hard in the back ... but when he looked around, no one was there. Another invisible man! It transpired that the farmer had attached his electric fence to Mr Blue's garden fence and the invisible punch that had so frightened William was, in fact, an electric shock. Needless to say, it took some time before William ventured back out into the garden to play!

To be honest, there are so many things that frighten me, not necessarily because they are frightening, but because I don't understand them. Every 'first' is a challenge to understand and overcome. Whether it be the radio, the TV, the toaster popping, the doorbell ringing, the smoke alarm going off, an alarm clock, the bang of a slamming door, my human sneezing or knocking something over or dropping something on the floor (which he does quite a lot), him cursing when a red car overtakes one of his beloved blue cars in something called motor racing; even the final shutting of a book after he has finished a story.

Make no mistake, I am loving my new life and I am beginning to understand that I am now safe, but that doesn't stop me jumping out of my fur almost every day. Any unexpected or unexplained noise or movement represents a fearful moment to me.

So, to those who say "Put him in a room with people and he'll have to learn to cope" I say "Please don't judge me as you would a domesticated dog".

Being a pet dog (as I now am) clearly isn't as dangerous as being a feral dog but, as the saying goes, you can take the dog out of the street but you can never take the street out of the dog!

I am who I am, and I always will be!

Chapter 32

An audience with Dame Polo

While writing my chapter on fear, I had a somewhat inspirational thought, why not call Dame Polo de la Soi, the grandee of all Soi Dogs, and ask her pawspective on the matter?

Somewhat recklessly, and without thinking my idea through, I dialled up Dame Polo on SnoutTime and was surprised to hear her phone answered by a human. "Dame Polo's residence, how can I help you?" a voice asked politely.

Rats, I cursed to myself, I should have given this more thought. How can I explain that I need to talk with Dame Polo when I only speak Woof, and Thai Woof at that?

"I have a feeling that maybe you want to talk with Dame Polo?" the voice suggested. "If so you'll need to tell me what this is all about as she can't take calls from just anyone you know." It seemed to me that the voice had just become a tad sterner!

I was in trouble. If only I could tell her that I was a Soi Dog, I mused, it might just help.

"Ah" said the voice softening, "You wouldn't be a Soi Dog by any chance? I have a feeling that you are! Well I am afraid that Dame Polo is out hunting Pat the Twat right now and won't be back until later."

I had heard about Pat the Twat on social media and I knew that he was a cat who lived next door to Dame Polo. But I also knew that Pat the Twat had moved house quite recently and I groaned to myself, thinking that this might be something of a fob-off.

"You're rather well informed young pup" said the voice, beginning to sound quite friendly. "But you should know that cats often return to their former homes, so Dame Polo is busy setting a trap just in case the Twat returns". The voice chuckled heartily at this suggestion. "By the way, my name's Donna and I am Dame Polo's private secretary. Who are you, if I may ask?".

By now I was beginning to wish that I had asked my human to make this call for me. He could have explained that I was Mr Knight, recently from Phuket, even though I somehow doubted that Donna would have heard of me.

"Mr Knight? The Mr Knight? Yes, of course, we know all about you. Dame Polo is an avid reader of the Soi Dog Post. Well, under the circumstances, I am quite sure that she would be delighted to take your call if you phone back this afternoon at 16:00. No earlier mind you, as one of the Royal Corgis has been pestering us for weeks now. He's desperate for Dame Polo's pawtograph and insists that it's for his human who is a huge fan and, apparently, a rather impawtant person. So goodbye for now, but don't forget to call back later!"

The line went dead and that was it, my SnoutTime with Dame Polo was set in stone.

They say that some things are easier said than done and, suddenly, I realised the enormity of what was about to happen. I had set up a SnoutTime meeting with THE Dame Polo de la Soi who had lived with St Gill and St John and now lived with Donna. While Donna described herself as Dame Polo's PA, I was unnerved to hear from my human that she was actually the President of Soi Dog UK. Was I out of my depth? And just who was I to phone Dame Polo out of the blue and ask for an interview? How would she react to me?

I'm smiling at the memory now, but it is just as well I didn't know what was coming, as I might well have chickened out! I guess you don't become a Dame for nothing in this world and Dame Polo certainly proved to be otherworldly! At exactly 16:00 I called back and Donna replied, "Perfect timing Mr Knight as Dame Polo has just finished her call ... it seems that she has quite a fan club, but that's another story! Anyhow, she's expecting your call so I'll put you through right now".

It is fair to say that I knew Dame Polo would be different, but I certainly wasn't expecting this:

DAME POLO: "Yo! Knight Boy, how's it hangin? Dame Polo De La Soi speaking to you loud and clear, person to person, snout to snout from sunny Hornsea where it's 90° in the shade 52 weeks a year.

"Now boy ... before I kick off, just remember that time is money, so don't expect to make a meal of this interview. I trust you've spoken to my PA regarding fees? I don't normally discuss financials myself as I consider it uncouth BUT ... suffice to say I did a spread for Hello Magazine last week entitled 'There is nothing like a Dame' and they are paying me a considerable amount in cash. Mum has probably explained to you that we both have issues with HMRC so it's cash only for this job please and thank you!"

Who would have guessed it, a real hip-hop Dame in the Soi Dog family! Fortunately I had prepared some questions in advance and, somewhat hesitantly, I kicked off with my first question.

ME: "Um, err, I understand you were rescued as a pup. What happened to you?"

DAME POLO: "Not something I like to talk about really as I started my life anew once my paws hit Blighty, but I'm all for a bit of drama and attention so here goes.

"I was very poorly indeed, you name it, I had it all ... blood parasites, severe mange and malnutrition and I had honestly lost every ounce of will to live. I was stuck alone in a place where many people, including European tourists saw me yet ignored me and walked on by.

"Some very cruel humans threw things at me, sticks and stones, like I was target practice because I could not move through sheer weakness and just being too poorly to go on. I was only seven months old, totally alone and bewildered, frightened at who was going to kick or hit me with something next. I was grabbing at any passing cockroach just to get some protein in me, but the thirst in the Thai heat was agonising. I need to move on from this subject as it makes me hungry."

ME: "Oh, okay, er ... how long did you live at Soi Dog?"

DAME POLO: "I never stayed at the shelter. The shelter is for strays, not Dames. I looked Gill Dalley firmly in the eye and told her that if she wanted me off the streets I would only go with her if she took me home. She knew we were kindred spirits and that I meant business. Gill took me into the old hospital at the shelter most days and gave me baths of some awful, stinky stuff that stung my skin but I trusted her so went along with it. She would bathe me then wrap me up in a big white towel like the Baby Jesus himself, then kiss me on my nose.

"Everyone says I have attitude because my Mum is the same, but it's Gill who started me off with my delusions of grandeur and now it is second nature.

"I miss Gill terribly. Mum and I started a wall of remembrance at the shelter in Gill's honour. The first plaque went up from us to Gill on the day of Gill's funeral."

Dame Polo had slipped into a more reverent mode while talking about St Gill, but my very next question brought her back to normality!

ME: "When and how did you come to England?"

DAME POLO: "December 2013 on an aeroplane, you cat-for-brains! I'm a good swimmer, but I'm not that good! We flew into Amsterdam and then took the ferry to Harwich, followed by a long drive up to Yorkshire. Gill and John call Yorkshire 'God's own country' and who am I to disagree. I love it up here".

I couldn't get used to her over-familiar reference to St Gill and St John, but I ploughed on regardless.

ME: "How long did it take you to settle into your new life?"

DAME POLO: "Immediately. It was easier for me than for some because I knew my Mum as she was Gill's best friend. Rather cleverly, she always smelt of Gill as she wore her t-shirts to cuddle and reassure me."

So far I was edging around the fear issue, trying to win Dame Polo's trust, but the time had come to start asking the really difficult questions.

ME: "What frightens you?"

DAME POLO: "How long have you got, Knight Boy? Here's a list for starters: ladders; blind men's sticks; serial killers; Pablo the Spanish vet; people who stamp their feet (I could never watch Riverdance); unpredictable people; smoke alarms; people who talk loudly; fisherman's hooks (I nearly choked on a scabby bit of mackerel attached to one); delivery men; Donald Trump - I make a rule of never discussing religion or politics but someone bought Mum a life size cut-out of The Donald for her office and it fell on me once; footballs and most of all Mum's suitcase and overnight bag. I hate it when they come out of the wardrobe."

Clearly this was a subject that Dame Polo found difficult to talk about, hence her somewhat tongue in cheek answer. So I reluctantly pushed further.

ME: "How do you react to fear, what do you do?"

DAME POLO: "I bite and you can take that as a threat, Knight Boy! It's normally a nip and run as I'm scared deep down, but don't tell that to Pat the Twat. My therapist told me that my behaviour is called 'Fear Aggression'. When I get scared, I get a build up of adrenaline and this has to be released somehow ... usually by barking or by attacking another dog although, to be honest, I very rarely bite. You know the expression "Her bark is worse than her bite", well that's me all over!"

ME: "Do you ever think that you'll fully relax when out and about?"

DAME POLO: "Not really, but I'm happy if my Mum is there as she understands me. I also have an Aunty Karen who I trust being out with and a special Uncle."

Remembering my own occasional nightmares, I probed further.

ME: "Do you have nightmares or flashbacks?"

DAME POLO: "Do I have nightmares Knight Boy? I have night terrors! My Mum has to wake me up as I verge on fitting. It takes a long time to wake me and if I am allowed to go straight back to sleep, I go straight into another nightmare, so I normally have a bowl of milk to help me forget. I don't wet the bed though ... let's make that clear to the readers."

I thought that I had pushed far enough on the fear front, so I changed direction somewhat.

ME: "What do you prefer, humans or dogs?"

DAME POLO: "My Mum. My Granny. Karen. My special Uncle and John Dalley. I preferred Gill to all of the above but she passed away ..."

This comment was followed by a long silence, before Dame Polo continued:

"I don't understand this but my Mum says that one day I will meet Gill again. She will wrap her arms around me and we will kiss and be together until my Mum joins us. I also have a sister (not blood) called Martha. She's a Staffy and in my opinion, though not diagnosed, is special needs. Martha adores me ... I tolerate her. So, in the main I prefer people, but ONLY if I know them."

The interview was moving away from fear, but Dame Polo was speaking her mind and I was really enjoying the education.

ME: "What do you think of designer dogs?"

DAME POLO: "I think that lots of people judge rescue dogs

and mixed breed dogs based on the misconception that we are vicious or we all have behavioural problems, but that's not true. Like humans, some are naughty, some are good, some are nasty and some are gentle. I do think adopting a dog or cat is the kindest thing, because the shelters worldwide are full of homeless animals. Why would you encourage anyone to breed more dogs, besides, do lady dogs even enjoy doing 'it'? (I blushed at this point, thinking back to my earlier life in Phuket. Mindful that we were on SnoutTime, this was somewhat embarrassing and I received a rather stern look from Dame Polo). I know it's not for me, I much prefer an ice cream to be honest!

"Obviously I'm biased but I'd thoroughly recommend adopting a Soi Dog. There can be no comparison to what dogs go through in some parts of Asia, particularly within the barbaric Dog Meat Trade. Besides that, if you rescue one dog, you are making room for another to be saved so it really is a no-brainer. We just know that you saved our life, so we are loyal until the end."

I felt that my time was almost up, but I had two final questions to ask.

ME: "Is it true that you work for a living?"

DAME POLO: "Head Of Security, Soi Dog Marketing in Hornsea, Yorkshire. No pay, no perks, sometimes cold but worth it when an unsuspecting Yorkshire Terrier strolls past the window and doesn't see me lurking behind the orange bunting! There's no canteen and my Mum won't let me join a Union, but I am allowed to take my dinner in to work and we also feed hedgehogs in the car park, so sometimes I steal their food too".

ME: "May I ask when you became a Dame?"

DAME POLO: "Yo Knight, it's like this Boy. I proclaimed myself a Dame when I was immortalised in the bronze statue of Gill holding me which stands at the shelter. I actually thought that being a Dame meant I would be able to get things free, like shopping and Amazon Prime, but all it really means is that the locals have to curtsy when they see me pass by. John (Dalley) and my Mum will be going to collect his MBE at Windsor Castle soon and I wonder if John will feel as important as I do? I also worry that my Mum will end up in the Tower Of London as she, like me, is quite the anarchist. I know for a fact that she's only going along for a free sandwich and I'm hoping that she snaffles me a few cocktail sausages from the finger buffet; or even some of that Royal Corgi dog food. I've actually been angling at an invite to the ceremony, but those Corgis are clearly threatened by a Dame!

"Hey Knighty Boy. Remember that fee I threatened you with earlier. I was only joking about paying me cash ... "

ME: "Wow, thank you", I exclaimed.

DAME POLO: "I haven't finished yet, Boy. I don't want the money, but I'm not letting you off the hook. You can pay my fee to the Gill Dalley Memorial Fund for Disabled Animals instead."

ME: "Err yes, absolutely and thank you for ..."

But the line had already gone dead and Dame Polo's image had disappeared from my screen. I imagined her sitting back with Donna, having a giggle at my expense, but despite this, a broad smile spread over my face. Me, a mere street dog from Phuket, had just had a 15 minute SnoutTime with the world famous Dame Polo de la Soi. Ma Knight would have been so proud!

Chapter 33

Mid-term progress report

I must say, I am very happy with my human's training and, although I say it myself, I think he is coping very well with his new life.

We live in a period house set within 800 acres of National Trust land, meaning that we have a vast choice of walks on our doorstep. That said, the garden around my house is communally owned by the 15 households on the estate and it's all open plan, so I don't have a private garden to roam around in when I take the fancy.

Walking with my human is an interesting experience. You will remember from the initial walks I had with him in the Sanctuary, that he talks to me as he walks which I like, as I find his voice very soothing and reassuring.

He is also very patient, which is just as well as I like my smells. Sometimes, after I've stopped to sniff my 50th rabbit hole, he might gently tug on the lead and say something like; "Come on old boy, we've come out for a walk, not a sniff"!

My favourite walks are first thing in the morning and last thing at night, as these are the times we go exploring. These are my "hunting" walks and, although I have yet to catch a rabbit or squirrel, I've been very close on numerous occasions. It's during these walks that we have the most fun as we spend much of the time running, certainly until my legs start to ache. Two-legs lets me take the lead, so I dictate the speed and duration of any sudden dash towards a potential bonus meal.

Sometimes I stop suddenly to smell something and human (who is always close by) has to jump over me to prevent a collision. On these occasions he sometimes falls over when he lands and this is followed by much groaning and even cursing! He then grins and says something along the lines of: "For God's sake dog, how about some paw signals to let me know when you're stopping" and then he guffaws. I want to reply something along the lines of "But I did make poor signals" but my English is not that good and I am worried that I might mix up my paws with my pores, or pours or even pause! To be honest, I have no idea what all this chatter really means but human clearly likes it and thinks it's funny, so I make a point of suddenly stopping on every walk we take to keep him happy.

In the colder weather when the ground is wet and slippery, he sometimes forgets to put on his wellies and this results in him slip-sliding about. Sometimes I look at him in sympathy and he mutters words along the lines of: "It's okay for you, you've got four-paw drive, but I'm all over the place in these conditions". This is another comment that always brings a big smile to his face, so I make a point of leading him into a muddy, slippery place whenever he's wearing normal shoes!

I've said that my human likes talking during walks, and this includes to every other walker, especially if they have a dog. He calls most dogs "monster" or "beautiful" and, in the main, they seem to like him. The human to human conversation usually comes around to my scars at some stage and my human then tells the tale of Soi Dog and my rescue and rehabilitation. I never tire of this story, for while it was terrifying at the time, I now know that, without Soi Dog, I would not be alive ... and enjoying three to four walks a day!

My human calls all this chit-chat "socializing" and he repeatedly explains to me how important it is, although I am not sure whether it is important for him or for me. Often I find myself growling at the other humans' dogs although, as I get to know them better, I find that there's more to talk about.

Although most humans still scare me, some of the humans that my human talks to are very kind and, much to my surprise, I find my tail wagging furiously when I see these people.

The first to win me over was Graham who had two small dogs, Polo and Piglet. When my human first met him, Graham was wearing a Haywards Heath Rugby Club shirt and, as my human explained, you can't get better than a rugby player who loves dogs. Although I had no idea what this meant, I took an immediate liking to Graham. To my surprise, I completely forgot to be timid!

Next, and much to human's delight, we befriended Claire and Izzy and their dog Pepper. This was a very special meeting as Pepper is also a Soi Dog ... what a coincidence! The village that we live in has a population of under 1000 people ... and it has TWO Soi Dogs. As you can imagine, Pepper and I had much to talk about; no growling between the two us!

I need to mention a few more human friends. Most days we see another Graeme and he also has two dogs, Maurig (the dark one) and Ollie. Maurig is very lively and always jumps up at my human but I just ignore this as Graeme usually has a bit of ham in his pocket for me which is more important! We also meet three huge Alsatians called Olly, Evie and Jay. Olly sometimes barks at me, but the one thing I am used to is barking dogs, so I tend to ignore him and he quietens down. My human always says "Hello Monsters" to them, but I know he likes them very much. They are walked by Pat and Lisa who always give me special treats ... so I really like them too.

Then there's Michael and Daisy who we meet on our early morning walks. I really like Michael as he is very kind to me. He is my favourite walking friend and I also like the treats he gives me! Daisy is twice the size of me and very blonde, she is half Husky and half German Shepherd. Usually she is busy jumping into muddy puddles, so I don't know her very well, but we are slowly becoming friends. Just recently I've been teaching her to hunt and she's been encouraging me to join her in the undergrowth for a bit of a run around. Michael and my human laugh at this and mutter words along the lines of "Mr Knight was such a nice young pup until he met Daisy, but he's so easily led astray!".

Finally there is Vicky, the most important of all my walking friends. My human calls her Plan B, which is a strange name to call someone called Vicky but, as I have learned, my human is a bit strange. Anyhow, Vicky walks me regularly, usually twice a week, and we often go out with other dogs in a pack, my favourites being Max and Bella. Vicky understands me really well, maybe because she also walks Soi Dog Pepper. Sometimes, when it is wet and cold outside, we play games indoors and she whispers: "Let's stay nice and warm today, Mr Knight. Your dad can take you out when he gets back"; then she laughs!

I'm not sure what my human does when Vicky comes over. I think he must go hunting as he always returns with food, albeit strange looking food, wrapped up in bags and boxes. My human doesn't eat meat and he doesn't allow others to eat meat in his house, but he makes an exception for me. So, when off hunting he always brings home a chicken. Well, at least I think it's a chicken; it certainly smells like a chicken and tastes a bit like one; but it doesn't look like one as it doesn't have feathers or a head.

My human says that if people had to kill their own meals, they might think twice about what they eat. I don't know what this means, but it must be a very important message as he always looks so sincere when he says it.

Back to walking. When I first arrived, as you will remember, I was terrified to go out and, every time I saw a human out on a walk, I would dive into the nearest bush and try desperately to escape. Happily my human understood this and we spent a lot of time together in the undergrowth. Sometimes human growled if there were prickle bushes, but he never once made me talk to someone when I was scared.

This helped me build my confidence and now I am beginning to realise that most humans are kind and represent no danger to me.

I don't think that I will ever be completely relaxed in the company of strangers, but I have made many good friends during my walks, from both two-legged and four-legged packs and my life is very much the better for these encounters.

Walking is definitely the best part of my day, although I do also like curling up on my sofa and snoozing next to my human. Mr Blue has told me that, one day, I will be able to run around outside without my lead, but first he has to be sure that I won't run away. Run away? Why would I do that?

Chapter 34

Christmas in England

I have now been living in England for almost five months and I was beginning to understand the pattern of my life. It seemed to me that there were five days when my human was a bit subdued, followed by two days when he was really happy, followed by five more subdued days etc. This pattern aligned with going to the office and weekends and, needless to say, I always preferred the two day highs. But suddenly things changed and every day became a high!

I don't fully understand what I am about to explain but one day my human said to me "No more work for the next two weeks Knighty Knight as Christmas is coming!" and he said this with the biggest of smiles on his face. "Now we need to go and find ourselves a Christmas tree" and with that he harnessed me up and off we set.

Ha ha, what an adventure that was! Usually it is me that stops every minute or so to explore the multitude of smells that I come across on walks but on this particular day it was my Mr Blue who was darting left, right and centre; exploring every fallen branch and every twig he saw lying on the ground.

Now I vaguely remember 'Christmas trees' from my time at Soi Dog. Once a year an extremely lush green tree would appear at the sanctuary with a big sign attached to it saying NO PEEING ON THIS TREE. Needless to say, this same tree became the most peed upon tree on earth for a few weeks before it wilted and gave up the ghost! What else would you expect of 800 dogs and a sign that said NO PEEING?!

So why were we looking for twigs and branches, rather than a full blown tree? Well, part of the answer is because my human is a non-conformist ... even I had noticed how odd he was! But I had also discovered that Curvy Two-Legs was due to spend Christmas with us and Curvy is an artist, so my human was trying very hard to be artistic!

Curvy, as you will all remember, is my rival for Mr Blue's affection. It had been a while since she had last visited and my human was determined to put on a good show for her. The trouble was, I wasn't really helping because, every time he pointed at a fallen branch, I would go over and pee on it! In time we found just what he was looking for ... an off-cut from a rather sad looking Silver Birch sapling. I was just about to pee on it when human wailed "Noooooo Knight" and with that he picked it up and admired it lovingly. "Just what we want" he said cradling the bald branch. I tut-tutted, as much as a dog can tut-tut, and decided to go along with his little fantasy! Back home, I chose to have a short power nap while my human set about decorating his rather forlorn looking tree. I was vaguely aware of contented humming in the background while I snoozed but, when I awoke, I must confess I gasped ou loud!

In the corner of the room, looking quite magnificent, stood our Christmas tree, covered in gold and red glittery balls, slivers of gold and red tape and a dog with wings perched on the top! "Watch this Knighty" said my human and, with that, he flicked a switch and the whole tree started to glow. "Happy almost Christmas, beautiful" said Mr Blue, then he leant over and kissed me.

That evening Curvy Two-Legs arrived wearing a funny red hat with a white bobble, full of laughter and laden with presents. Much to my surprise, I found myself chasing my tail and acting in a very puppy-like fashion; I was just so excited.

"Hello Wagalot" said Curvy with a huge smile on her face, "we're going to have so much fun this Christmas, aren't we!" and then out of nowhere, she produced a delicious treat for me.

Next she went over to Mr Blue and ... well I averted my eyes for a few seconds so as to avoid any embarrassment. Yes, there was a magical feeling around and about the house; Curvy was glowing, my human was glowing, the living room was glowing, the tree was glowing; and so was I!

Of course a dog must do what a dog must do and so, before settling down for the evening, Curvy and Mr Blue wrapped up well and took me out for a Christmas Eve walk. While there was no snow, the air was crisp and the ground was dry underfoot, so I knew that I would get a nice long walk. When out and about I often study my human as he is so different to me and this evening I was intrigued to see him look up towards the heavens and mouth the words "Happy Christmas, dad" into the night sky. I wondered what this meant and so I looked up into the sky myself and saw that it was full of beautiful, gleaming stars, just like our Christmas tree. Then I remembered that all our departed friends turned into stars and I found myself wondering which one of the millions of stars above might be my friend Daengseed.

At that very moment I felt, rather than heard, her ethereal voice speaking to me, oh so sweetly, "Well done Knight, my dearest of friends. You have certainly honoured your promise of all those months ago and I can tell you now that you will be forever happy."

Suddenly it seemed to me that two stars in the sky were shining just a little bit brighter than all the others and with huge joy I realised that I knew whose stars they were. One was my dear friend Daengseed and the other was St Gill, who designed the Soi Dog hospital that saved my life. Next to St Gill's star was a very faint glow, another star in the making, but not yet ready to shine. I thought of Soi Dog and of all the animals that St John had saved, and I prayed to the Gods above that they might delay the lighting of his star for a few more years to come.

"Happy almost Christmas everyone" Mr Blue called out to anyone we passed by and my thoughts returned to earth. Me, my human and Curvy were walking in this beautiful place in peace and in complete safety. "Happy Woofmas, sweet Daengseed" I whispered as we turned around and headed for home.

Christmas is indeed a magical time and while we had been out walking, piles of beautifully wrapped presents had mysteriously appeared under our tree. I noticed that some of them were bone shaped and I found myself wondering what they could possible be. "I bet you can't guess what those ones are" said Mr Blue with a grin and then he and Curvy told me a somewhat fantastical story. An old dog called Woofalot Woofmas, so they said, visited every house over Christmas to deliver presents to good dogs and, somewhat bizarrely, he came down the chimney rather than in through the front door. Now I knew that this couldn't possibly be true as we didn't have a chimney, although we did have a fireplace of sorts as Curvy had programmed the TV to show a crackling log fire on the screen. The whole story seemed highly implausible to me, but I didn't mind as it was Christmas and I was beginning to believe that anything was possible.

"You must be hungry!" said Mr Blue suddenly. I don't know whether he was talking to me or to Curvy but that didn't matter as Curvy was no longer my rival, she was my friend. He then proceeded to put on a very strange looking white hat with the words TRAINEE CHEF emblazoned on it and announced that he was going to cook dinner.

Curvy had had a long day travelling and Mr Blue suggested that she might like a short nap while he got on with his TRAINEE CHEF duties. Happily for me this included preparing my dinner which seemed to be just a little bit special on this most special of evenings. To be honest, cooking and my human do not usually go hand in hand. We used to have a smoke alarm in the kitchen but we had to remove it as it was always going off and frightening me. To replace it, he had bought a sign saying "Dinner is served when the smoke alarm goes off" which made everyone laugh ... except for me as I knew that it was true!

In time Curvy came down and I hardly recognised her as she was dressed most peculiarly in green and red. Indeed, if I didn't know better I might have thought that she was an elf but she smelt like Curvy, so I knew she had to be Curvy. I'm not sure that Mr Blue knew who she was as he just stood there staring, with his mouth gaping wide open! "Happy Christmas, luv" said Curvy and my human burst out laughing. "Wow, you look amazing" he spluttered, "this certainly calls for a bottle of fizz and a dog treat, don't you think Knighty Knight?" in answer to which I wagged my tail furiously.

Later that evening, after dinner and much frivolity, the three of us relaxed on the sofa together. While my human and Curvy discussed their plans for tomorrow, my first ever Christmas in England, I found myself pondering the almost unbelievable journey that had brought me from a near-death experience in Phuket Town to here, curled up on a sofa between Mr Blue and Curvy Two-Legs.

I thought about my many friends at Soi Dog's Gill Dalley Sanctuary and especially about those who had saved my life and given me new hope. Although, in many ways it seemed like a lifetime ago, it was but a year since I had first met Mr Blue; and I found myself praying that other dogs like me might soon find their own forever homes too.

I used to have nightmares, indeed I still do, but now when I awake, Mr Blue is always there; holding me, gently stroking me and telling me that I am safe. Honestly, could there ever be a luckier dog than me?

I really do hope that you have enjoyed my extraordinary but very true story. If you have, perhaps you too could find it within your heart to adopt a dog like me?

I am sure there are many tales that I have forgotten to tell, but please forgive me, as now I need to sleep.

Since I met my human I have had so much joy in my life, with many magical moments, but I just know that tomorrow is going to be the happiest day of my new life ... and I want to be ready.

www.soidog.org/adopt-a-dog

Chapter 35

The final word (written by my human)

Curtis Brown is a handsome man. He is tanned, muscular, extremely fit and sports a fine array of tattoos. In short, he looks pretty tough, not the sort of guy you would want to mess with!

On 28 December 2019 I sat down with Curtis to learn more about the crucial role played by his Behaviourist team at Soi Dog.

"What in particular would you like to know?" asked Curtis politely (for he is a quite delightful fellow).

"Well", I replied "in addition to understanding the role of your team at Soi Dog, I would also like to ask your advice on introducing a street dog to a house; as I have just adopted a dog called Knight."

Complete silence. No reply at all.

I looked up from my note book expectantly and to my amazement Curtis had welled up and had tears in his eyes. This extraordinary man, who would not have looked out of place leading the England XV on to the rugby pitch at Twickenham, was completely overwhelmed. Happily for me, he was overwhelmed with joy!

At the time of applying to adopt Mr Knight, I had absolutely no idea of what he had been through and that he was a seriously damaged dog, both physically and mentally; although his scars were a give-away to the former.

As you will have read in Mr Knight's own story, it was Curtis who gave Knight new life. Yes, the team in the Soi Dog hospital did a wonderful job of repairing his body (and for that we will both be forever grateful) but it was Curtis who spent an hour or more every day over a nine month period, helping Knight come to terms with humans. Mindful that Soi Dog cares for up to 800 dogs at any one time, and that a number of these dogs need special attention from Curtis and his team, then it is fair to say that the time Curtis spent with my boy Knight was nothing short of a labour of love.

Thank you Curtis. You will forever remain in Knight's heart.

Had I known at the time that Knight was such a traumatised dog, I might not have considered adopting him, but thank goodness I did because the experience of introducing Knighty into my life in England has been quite wonderful. To see Mr Knight gain confidence, very slowly as first and then in leaps and bounds (well mini-leaps and mini-bounds) has, at times, been overwhelming.

In fairness to Soi Dog, both Curtis and the Adoptions team went to great lengths to fill me in on Knight's back-story and the challenges that would lie ahead. These were very open and honest conversations and, on more than one occasion, I was presented with a no-loss-of-face get out of jail option. But, the more I heard of Knight's past, the more I wanted to be instrumental in securing his future!

To anyone thinking of getting a dog, I would urge you to adopt a rescue dog rather than to buy a puppy. There are thousands of very beautiful, healthy rescue dogs in shelters as I write these words, all desperate for a home ... and all desperate for love. Some are young pups and some are fully grown dogs, some are scared and some are full of confidence and raring to go. Puppies are only puppies for a few months, but a dog is a dog for a lifetime. And it is a dog that is Man's Best Friend.

The rewards to us humans of rescuing a dog that might otherwise have to be destroyed are immeasurable and my adoption of Mr Knight has been a rollercoaster of quite wonderful emotions.

Unlike Mr Knight, I am no author and, of some things, no man can write.

Suffice to say, most evenings I simply gaze in wonderment as Knighty snuggles down on our sofa before going to sleep. I look at him all curled up and perfect and I struggle to connect his past to his present. But his past was very real ...

Soi Dog rescued Mr Knight, I simply adopted him; and in so doing I filled my world with love of the very purest kind.

You are a miracle Mr Knight, may you lead a long and happy life.

#adoptdontshop

MR KNIGHT's THANK YOUs

To Curtis Brown without whom I would not have survived this ordeal.

To Gill and John Dalley, not only for my life, but also for the lives of hundreds of thousands of soi dogs and cats across Asia.

To Sam McElroy for being Sam. A man so full of enthusiasm, who cannot do enough to help me and my human.

To all the Soi Dog doctors who helped save my life in 2018, including Dr Ala, Dr Bow, Dr Sai, Dr Kate, Dr Parn, Dr Hope, Dr Ohm, Dr Su, Dr Nes, Dr Sprite and most notably Dr Eed, my surgeon.

To all the wonderful nurses at the Soi Dog hospital including my human's friend, Disney Sarah.

To Khun Eve, Mr O and all the Behaviourists for helping me find the will to live.

To Khun Doe and all the carers in the A runs. We all owe you so much.

To Gina, Laura, Linn and Sam H for organising my adoption and travel.

To Louise Rose for being the best boss of the best team in the whole world.

To Sarah Collier for delivering me into my new world in such a gentle and caring fashion.

To Donna Freelove for agreeing to look after me should anything ever happen to my human.

To my editors, Sheelagh Wrench and Caroline Peacock, for all their help. For the sake of authenticity, we have agreed to retain a number of my grammatical errors!

To Duncan Taylor-Jones for designing this beautiful book and for keeping an eye on my human!

To Scarlett Wrench and Celia Barstow for a final read-through, and for accepting my bad grammar with good humour.

To my human for painstakingly and patiently translating my Thai Woof ramblings to English. I know that we have jumped from present to past to future tense a few too many times, possibly even in the same sentence, but this is my first attempt at writing, so please forgive me.

And finally to Daengseed, the best friend a dog could ever have.
May you rest in peace.